Queen of the Track

Also by Adrianne Blue

Grace Under Pressure:
The Emergence of Women in Sport

Field Events

Faster, Higher, Further:
Women's Triumphs and Disasters at the Olympics

(with Fatima Whitbread)
Fatima: the Autobiography

Queen of the Track

The Liz McColgan Story

ADRIANNE BLUE

H. F. & G. WITHERBY LTD

First published in Great Britain by
H. F. & G. WITHERBY LTD
14 Henrietta Street, London WC2E 8QJ

A catalogue record for this book is available from
the British Library

ISBN 0 85493 223 2

Photoset in Great Britain by
Rowland Phototypesetting Ltd, Bury St Edmunds, Suffolk
and printed in Great Britain by
Mackays of Chatham plc, Chatham, Kent

For Deryck

Contents

Illustrations

Michael Aspel announces to an astonished Liz, 'This is
    Your Life'
With Yvonne Murray at Meadowbank, 1992
Defeated at the world cross-country championships.
    Boston, 1992
Liz leading the pack in the Barcelona Olympic final
A victory for African unity in the Barcelona Olympics

Acknowledgements

People who knew Liz McColgan when she was very young and who were present in Dundee as the events of her life unfolded have been generous with their recollections. I have often relied on their testimony, and want to thank in particular: Martin and Betty Lynch, Karen Beddows, Vi Bennett, Phil Kearns, Gail Pope McGregor, Barbara and Ron Oliver and Christine Price.

My thanks, too, for brief but very informative chats with Jean Tully, Andrew Smiley, Gordon Christie, Duncan Storey, 'Cookie', Caroline Smith, Kevin Lynch, Martin Lynch Jr and assorted Dundee taxi drivers.

Athletes and many other of the sport's insiders helped, in particular: Fatima Whitbread, Kirsty Wade, Paula Radcliffe, Lisa York, Yvonne Murray, Linford Christie, Steve Cram, Tony Ward, Nigel Whitefield, Joan Allison, Margaret Whitbread, John Mitchell, John and Dorothy Anderson and Andy Norman.

Sports correspondents and editors: Pat Butcher, Doug Gillon, Alan Hubbard, Duncan Mackay, Randall Northam and Cliff Temple. Thanks also to: *Athletics Today, Athletics Weekly, Today's Runner, Nexus, This Is Your Life*, BBC Scotland, the *Dundee Courier & Advertiser*, the *Scotsman, The Sunday Times*, the *New York Times*, the *Alabama Crimson-White* and to any other newspapers from which I may have quoted.

Of my other colleagues and friends who helped: David Pallister, Hendrik Hertzberg, Michele B. Slung, Madeleine Harmsworth, Bob Campbell, Lawrence Specker, Lyn Allison and especially Richard Wigmore, Victoria Petrie-Hay, Robert Kirby and my agent Giles Gordon.

Using the methods of modern biography I have dramatized

events during races and elsewhere, never going beyond the bounds of statements made by the principals in interviews with me or with one of my colleagues, or the personal recollections of people present at the time the event occurred.

My thanks, too, to those who didn't want to be named, and to Liz McColgan whose deeds have inspired this book.

— 1 —

A Purely Personal Best

Her breasts hurt. Everything hurts. Her head down, the dark blonde hair pulled back into its characteristic tight topknot, running, Liz McColgan ignores the pain. On this raw December day, there is not much traffic on these winding country lanes. The few local drivers on their way to Dundee keep a careful eye out around the bends for Arbroath's most famous citizen because she doesn't watch out for them. Her eyes gaze steadily inward, aware only of her body, herself.

Even on fine days the scenery does not distract her: fields, trees, open skies and, further on, the swirling River Tay. Dundee-bound on a clear day, you can even glimpse the tip of St Andrews where Mary, Queen of Scots played golf in 1563. But the view doesn't tempt Liz, especially not today when every part of her feels so tender.

Just eleven days ago, on 25 November 1990, Liz Lynch McColgan gave birth to her first child. It was a difficult birth, following a forty-eight-hour labour. Her athlete's stomach muscles, which were expected to assist the baby in its exit, were in her case, she was told, *too* strong. 'My pelvic muscles were so tight, the baby couldn't get her head through.'

When, finally, the midwife at Ninewells Hospital put the seven pound thirteen and a half ounce perfect baby on to the scales, Liz and her husband Peter, a blue-eyed, darkly handsome Northern Irelander, called their daughter Eilish, which is Irish for Elizabeth.

Most women give it at least six weeks before they return to serious running. Even that stubborn sprinter Gwen Torrence, whose crack Georgia team Liz used to race against when they were both elite student athletes in America, gave it a month and could only last eight minutes on her first run. Well, Liz has always been a woman in a hurry. Now bundled into several warm layers, under which even after her pregnancy she is hungry-looking, Liz is out there on her first training run. She would have gone out running before, she confides to the ever-inquisitive press, but 'I was bloody sore, I could hardly walk.' Nor could she sit down.

But she could try to run.

Now she is running. One mile. Two miles. A paltry amount. Hurting everywhere, running before the stitches are out, she forces herself on. Her usual morning training run this time of year is closer to fifteen miles. In the weeks preceding a marathon it will go nearer twenty. Just one more more mile. Liz keeps going. Ignoring the pain.

What does she focus on as she runs? Do her eyes ever see all the way back to that gawky twelve-year-old's scarey moment when a gang of boys chased and chased her down long paths and past thick clumps of bushes through Caird Park? Does she remember how she felt on top of the world when she outran them?

Does she think of Harry? Harry ran even though it hurt. Harry Bennett, if he were here now in his navy blue track suit and his baseball cap, would help. Without him she will do what Harry used to call out to her to do when she was twelve, thirteen, fourteen years old, and losing steam as she ground up one more diabolical Dundee hill.

'Liz, you can do it,' Harry, her coach, would shout down at her from atop the steep brae where he was waiting for her. 'Rely on your superior strength!'

Aye. She will. Relying on her superior strength, she will pound out three miles today, three miles again tomorrow, five miles the next day, and on the fourth day ten.

As she runs does Liz ever recall the unexpected exhilaration of her first great triumph? Or is it the relatively depressing state of her bank balance that engages her more? For most of the year Liz, the family breadwinner, has not been earning.

Finally, on one of the last days of 1990, but the first day of what will become Elizabeth McColgan's most miraculous year, she arrives home having completed the three miles she set out to do, aching. No world-beater today, not a record-breaker, but a runner achieving a purely personal best. She is determined to go the distance again tomorrow. Despite the pain.

Why? Is she a masochist, or possessed by a magnificent obsession? Or is there something else that makes Liz McColgan run? Something more than the porridge and prunes she breakfasts on at home in Woodfield House's exquisitely fitted kitchen. Something more than the slices of Mother's Pride white bread which, so the advertisement beneath Liz's picture on the clear plastic package asserts, 'I grew up eating'?

Liz has a dream.

Her heart's desire is to become the world's greatest distance runner. It is an unusual dream, one that has already given her *almost* everything a woman could wish for – fame, fortune and great personal happiness.

What few people know is that poverty and pain, scandalous controversy and hurt have stalked Liz all the way.

Her dream is what makes Liz McColgan run. One of the things that makes Liz McColgan run faster today is blue-eyed Eilish. Liz wants to make sure Eilish gets a more promising start in life than hers was.

— 2 —

Rich Little Poor Girl

Princess Margaret and the Earl of Snowdon would soon be going to the London film premiere of the Beatles' *A Hard Day's Night*. Mini-skirts were coming in and the mods were battling with the duck-tailed rockers when, on 24 May 1964, four weeks after the hip Princess had herself given birth to a daughter and two days before the typhoid outbreak in nearby Aberdeen, Betty Lynch bore her fourth child, a girl, Elizabeth.

Vi Bennett, a friend of Betty, describes her as 'a very bubbly, bouncy sort of person. She's very likeable, with lots of hair.' For years Betty, who worked in a pub as a barmaid, was the family breadwinner. Something about her, a down-to-earth liveliness, reminds me of my favourite *Neighbours* character, Madge.

Six months after the baby was born Mary Rand won Britain's first ever Olympic gold medal in women's athletics. Her room-mate at the Tokyo Olympic village, Ann Packer, soon added the 800-metre gold. Betty and her husband Martin took more interest in the Labour victory and the prospect of Harold Wilson as Prime Minister.

They were living in a tenement near a main road on a Dundee council estate. Martin, who felt he had left the RAF too late to learn a trade, was usually out of work. When he did work it was on the roads, but whatever he was doing he was incredibly good company.

When their baby became a toddler he and Betty worried about the traffic. 'In summer time,' Betty would nervously tell the millions of people viewing *This Is Your Life*, 'I had to tie a rope around her middle out on the green near the clothes line so she could go out and play, because if you didn't she went on to the road.'

Little Elizabeth Lynch grew up with a temper, and a decided unwillingness to be bound by what appeared to be her destiny. She also had a tomboy's instinct for survival, which she would certainly have to make use of in Whitfield.

The two worst council estates in Dundee had one thing going for them: St Saviour's. Poor, white, gang-besieged, the Fintry estate and its neighbouring Whitfield – the terrible twins, with their perennial plagues of high unemployment and unwanted pregnancies – needed any saviour they could get.

Unlike some of the previous generations of Catholic schools, St Saviour's, which was within walking distance of the two estates, was no repository of repression. Practically brand new, the one-storey school was too young to be hostage to hairshirt tradition, and many of the teachers were still young enough to care. Phil Kearns was one of them.

It was the autumn of 1976. Far away in London it would be two years before the sky darkened into the bleak winter of discontent. Up here discontent was what people lived with in all four seasons every year. Thirty-four-year-old Phil Kearns hoped there might be something he could do about it.

A year ago, he himself had suffered a great disappointment. Racing in the wrong shoes, Kearns, who had the long, slender bones and the lean frame that one often associates with runners, had ruptured his Achilles tendon. He had left it alone to heal by itself, and it hadn't healed properly.

Now he was facing up to the fact that he would never run in another marathon, nor ever experience the inner pleasure of lining up for a club race he could romp away with.

Kearns had never thought of himself as a tremendous talent but he had been good enough to have a proper coach, the fiercely garrulous Glaswegian John Anderson, who much later and much less happily would coach Liz McColgan. John Anderson, who was making a name for himself south of the border, had coached Kearns by post.

Now Kearns, who was still jogging nearly every day for up to

half an hour, would have to forget all that. He was the St Saviour's
PE teacher and he threw himself into his work which, of course,
was not limited to his classes in the gym.

From time immemorial teachers have monitored school hall-
ways. There one day Phil Kearns had to separate one of the
first-year girls from another girl she was fighting. Skinny little Liz
Lynch, who had been on the point of winning, glared up at him
angrily, the corners of her mouth turning down into that dour,
now famously defiant pout.

There was something particularly aggressive in this one, Kearns
decided. It would have to be channelled into something.

St Saviour's had its share of wee Bonnie and Clydes, but as
Phil Kearns, now the assistant head teacher, explains, 'kids in
every school have fist fights, especially when they are establishing
the pecking order.'

At the time Elizabeth Lynch entered the school, she was an
unruly twelve-year-old from an unruly estate. At first glance her
bushy, nearly blonde hair, which was usually tied into two
bunches, seemed the only thing disciplined about her. 'I was
better than they thought,' Liz reckons. At the time she had plenty
to fight about.

The Fintry and Whitfield estates – the Lynch family moved
from one to the other – were at the bottom of the pecking order.
Flat, grey, ill-conceived, these housing blocks, now largely
boarded up, promised their inhabitants little besides ugliness and
aggro.

'You had a lot to contend with because you came from Whitfield,' Liz's sister Karen, two years older, confides. 'Even
after you left school, if you said Whitfield, they said, "Oh God,
another one, she can't have any brains and she must be a tough
person." If you were going for a job you might not even be
considered.'

Children, we all know, can be even crueller than adults. Girls
were taunted because the estate they lived on had a high rate of
out-of-wedlock pregnancies. In the case of Liz Lynch, not only
was her father chronically unemployed but it was known her
mother worked late at night and as a barmaid. It is not hard to
imagine the unpleasant remarks that were sometimes hurled at

the two Lynch sisters. Few knew or cared what devoted parents Martin and Betty Lynch actually were.

You will find no bitterness in Liz. 'Och, it's no use being twisted up about life,' she realized long ago.

Kearns had taught all the Lynch children. Young Martin, the eldest, who was seven years older than Liz, had been a skilled long-jumper. Kevin, Martin's junior by three years, was the captain of the St Saviour's football team. He would grow up to play for second-division Arbroath and is now a Dundee police detective.

Liz's sister Karen, who had always been delicate, played netball but did not distinguish herself at PE. She felt unconfident about standing up for herself in a fight, which you often had to. At first Kevin looked out for both Liz and Karen, but when he left the school, where he had been one of the very first pupils, it fell to Liz.

'It was me who got into scrapes,' Karen recalls, 'her who sorted them out. Liz was a real tomboy. No fears of anything. Climbing trees, jumping. When we went swimming Liz dived like the boys did from the top board.'

'She was very boisterous,' Kevin adds. 'She used to run after us doing boyish things, climbing trees, football. My other wee sister didn't.'

Liz was a competitive little so and so. 'Outside, my daughter Elizabeth would always be racing around the block even against boys and that. I used to watch through the window,' recalls Martin Lynch, whose ulcers were one of the things that kept him unemployed. His lack of a sturdy trade in a rickety economy was the other. Since his wife was away at work, Martin kept an eye on their daughters.

'In these races the boy would run one way, Elizabeth would run the other and the winner would be the one who came round first. Nine times out of ten at that age my daughter would beat the boy.' There is something Ancient-Mariner-compelling about the way Martin Lynch nods that wispy thatch of thick grey hair and waves about his lit cigarette as he murmurs a story. If it is an epic incident in his daughter's saga you are spellbound.

Proud fathers don't get the press they deserve, but the Dundee newspaper's chief reporter says Martin Lynch, who used to ring the paper whenever Liz Lynch won *anything*, should be given a trophy as the world's proudest father. It was because of him that quite a few years after he started calling she first got her name in the *Courier*.

'My wee daughter was always wanting to do handstands, crabs and roll about the floor,' Martin continues. 'And she hated to be beat.' As a young child, if she didn't win, there would be temper tantrums.

'Even when I was five or six, playing table tennis with my brother, I played until I dropped,' Liz herself says. What she means is she played until she won. Slapping that little white ball back and forth across the big table which was set up in her and Karen's bedroom, young Liz would force Kevin to keep on playing until she was victorious.

Not gifted academically, she was utterly uninterested in schoolwork. 'She was in no trouble in school,' Phil Kearns says, 'but it was not for her, and she was short-tempered.'

A strong character, she didn't like to do what she didn't like to do. One of the things she didn't like to do was sit still.

'Teachers told me, "Liz, your brains are in your feet".'

In the staff room Phil Kearns begged to differ with the cynics. Her short fuse, her bounds of energy, were all to the good in PE. True, PE was the only thing at school Liz was good at, but Kearns-style PE was by no means an easy option.

Like the boys, Liz's class of first-year girls was expected to run a lap around the school grounds, which were extensive enough for Phil Kearns to have mapped out a meandering mile-long loop around their grassy perimeter. Despite its endemic poverty, Dundee has a wealth of green spaces even in the inner city, especially in comparison to London or New York. Pupils at St Saviour's saw grass, trees, wagtails, even gardeners' sheds. The run, which Phil Kearns jokingly referred to as the 'lap of honour', was required of every pupil at every session of PE.

'Some of the girls would hide behind the sheds and have a smoke,' Liz is amused to remember, 'but I used to love it.' With her long legs and big feet, gawky, colt-like, skinny little Liz –

who hated to be called Lizzie – often found herself in the lead.
She was fast.

What no one at St Saviour's had yet realized was that Liz really
liked to do what she did like to do, and that, it soon became
apparent, was running, which was the perfect channel for all that
excess vigour.

The annual Dundee Schools Championships were to take place
at St Saviour's. The course was over the same field on which Liz
and the rest of her class ran their daily PE lap of honour. The
difference was the opposition. Each school sent a team of its
fastest eight or ten girls.

Surrounded by 120 of the best Dundonian girl runners, an
unsmiling little Liz eyes up the opposition, so many of them
bigger than she. She glances, perhaps a trifle nervously, at her
shoelaces. This will be her first ever real race.

'Go!' suddenly claps the starter, and Liz puts her head down
and runs, round the lap of honour once, round the lap of honour
twice, not sure where the opposition or the finish is, but running,
going fast, when she hears someone calling after her. 'Liz,' shouts
her teacher, Mr Kearns, chasing behind her. 'Liz, you can stop
now, you've already crossed the finish line, the race is over and
you won.'

She'd won. It must have been a wonderful feeling.

Even for her father it was extraordinary: 'When I saw my wee
daughter win by well over a hundred metres, and against girls so
much taller than what Elizabeth was,' Martin Lynch remembers,
'I realized I had something special.'

Her teacher Mr Kearns did too. 'If you join a running club,
Liz, you can put more into it and get more out.'

Liz wasn't eager. Streetwise as a Whitfield girl had to be early,
she knew that just getting to the park where the club trained
would be far from simple.

'Liz, just go and try it, see what you think. I'll phone the
Hawkhill Harriers and let them know you're coming up. The
coach is Harry Bennett, who I used to run with of an evening
when I was in the Harriers myself.'

Then Kearns rang Harry.

'I said to Harry, "There's a lassie coming up. I'm trying to get her to go with another friend because she didn't want to go alone because from Whitfield to Caird Park means passing through country that is sort of a gang area. And going home it would be dark and that."'

Harry understood immediately. On late nights he would see to it that they had an escort at least part of the way home.

Harry in his North American baseball cap was standing near the edge of the cinder track when Liz, still only eleven, turned up with her school friend Kelly. Harry's wife Vi had bought the baseball cap for him when she was visiting her sister who had moved to Vancouver. It was Dundee Hawkhill Harrier colours, blue and white.

'Harry always wore that cap whenever he meant business,' recalls Vi, 'and when he was coaching he always meant business.'

None of their three sons was interested in athletics, but with his girl athletes Harry was something of a pied piper. He was known throughout Scotland for the fact that he had the right ideas about coaching young girls through the difficult years when many drop out, and he was careful with them to avoid burn-out. Then in his mid forties, with the sturdy build that would have suited him to rugby, Harry had the easy-going manner of a man who knows his words will be heeded. He needn't fight.

'Harry was an eight-hundred-metres runner, won the Scottish title,' reminds Liz. He and Vi had a cupboard full of china plates and dishes he had won as race prizes. It was legal for amateurs to be paid in ornate plates, perhaps because they were almost useless.

On Tuesday and Thursday evenings after work Harry, who was a press minder at D.C. Thomson & Co., the printers of *Beano*, would wash off the grease and the printer's ink, change into his blue track suit with the white stripe, tie on his trainers, and off he would go with his big pack slung across his big back to the fresh air of Caird Park.

'In that pack was everything you could think of, elastoplast, safety pins, extra warm clothing, whatever,' says Vi who helped stock it, 'in case the girls he was coaching got injured.' Harry had been coaching young Hawkhill Harriers for seven or eight years.

'The girls would come to the house and talk over their training.'

Vi hunches forward in the armchair in the same sitting room where a decade ago the girls used to watch their own running performances, camcorded by Harry, on the video. Not too many people were camcording unranked runners in those days. Maybe that is why he was beginning to be known for the excellence of his young racing 'stable'.

'One time the whole group, five of them, came over to watch *Chariots of Fire* on the video. They didn't even look up when I brought in the tea and orange drink.' This film, which spurred on a generation of runners, was even used for inspiration by that other famous athlete-mother Joan Benoit, an American, on the night before she won the first ever woman's Olympic marathon in Los Angeles.

As well as hundreds of club runners, Harry had trained a few who wore and won in Scottish and British international vests. It lent credence that he himself had once been a Scottish champion. Harry took his athletes as far as he could and then sent them to someone who could take them further.

At Caird Park, where young Liz and her school friend who seemed less willing had turned up for the training, Harry calmly put them through his standard paces. Some stretches, some laps. There were always other girls on the track training and before long all of them noticed Liz.

Caroline Smith, a few years older than Liz and a doctor's daughter, says, 'I remember this waif with a bandage on her knee; all legs, running fast.'

Barbara Oliver, the assistant coach, clearly recalls 'the child with her hair pulled firmly into bunches tied with ribbons, who was always on the move, hopping and skipping when she wasn't running.'

The first thing anyone noticed about Liz was that amazing energy. She seemed to be perpetually in motion. Gail Pope, aged nineteen, who was to become Liz's training partner some years later, was stationed as a race steward at a turning point in the route of a men's cross-country race in Caird Park when a skinny girl in the blue-and-white-quartered Hawkhill vest and running shorts came up to her to complain that she couldn't get on with her training, because of the race.

Before Gail could think of what to answer, some of the runners came by. 'It's off to the left,' Gail called.

'Aye.' Young Liz pointed, jumping up and down excitedly. 'Go left.'

'After that, she decided to hang about to yap and chat,' Gail Pope McGregor recalls. 'She stayed there with me, but she couldn't stay still. She jumped about, she was hopping all over the place, she was jumping. I thought, my God, she's like a jumping bean.'

In this high-strung girl running so awkwardly round his track, Harry Bennett sensed gargantuan potential. Elizabeth Lynch was not a beautiful runner, nor would she ever be. She was all protruding elbows and there was that hunched back, but she was a natural athlete and she loved to run. She had the lungs for it, and she had the heart: this one was full of determination. Harry could recognize quality when he saw it. He recognized it in little Liz.

Now it was Harry ringing Phil Kearns to say: 'I'm having a heck of a job to make sure the lassie isn't doing too much.'

'Harry was ahead of his time,' Kearns believes, 'in thinking children shouldn't do too much.'

'Harry was ahead of his time in everything,' Liz will tell you. 'He made it so much fun. We thought the exercises he gave us were just for fun, but they were all to strengthen our muscles.'

At a time when it was thought too many compliments would turn a child's head, Harry was always very encouraging.

'Harry could get the best out of anyone,' his wife Vi is by no means the only one to say. 'He would tell them to do it, and they would, to please him, and then they would find they had pleased themselves.'

Soon the moment that would matter most occurred. Liz took a look at Harry in his baseball cap, and saw a way forward. Harry looked at Liz and felt an intense desire to take her along the path. And that was that. They fell in love. Well, it was a sort of love, of the platonic variety, with that deep sense of commitment which coaches and athletes must feel if they are to achieve anything wonderful.

*

Before very long Liz's schoolmate dropped out, leaving Liz to make her own way to the park through the paved inner city jungle. Every time twelve-year-old Liz went to Caird Park for her athletics training she had to brave the no-man's land at the edge of the sullen Whitfield estate. It was so scarey that Liz contemplated giving up Harry and the Harrier training, but when she stopped for a while found she badly missed it.

It was in the park itself, though, that the gang of boys began to chase her. She ran as fast as she could. To the child beset by bullies who would do to her she did not know quite what, it must have seemed that she was running for her life. But they had picked on the wrong girl, hadn't they? When she eluded them the unconscious lesson surely was that running can save your life, Liz.

There was one other mishap which may have hindered any residual hopes that Liz or her mother or gran might have that she would still turn out to be as ordinary as anyone else.

It is her brother Kevin who has the clearest memory of the story: 'One time in sewing class, which Liz hated, she put a sewing needle through her finger.' The needle penetrated 'up the top of her nail'. Kevin was called out of his class to accompany her to the Dundee Royal Infirmary. 'We were driven in a car or taxi.' In shock, Liz was given a local anaesthetic 'and they hauled the needle out.'

Perhaps the unconscious lesson here was that sewing – doing ordinary girl's things – hurts.

Did these two childhood events pale into insignificance, as they might have with some girls, or did they become indelibly powerful triggering events, screen memories, which were buried deep in her psyche and would determine Liz Lynch in her course?

Apart from the negative, there was the very positive, the enthusiastic response at St Saviour's to her achievement. Immediately after her victory in the Dundee Schools Championship says Kearns, 'a wee medal' was thrust into Elizabeth Lynch's hands. Then her triumph was lauded for a second time at a prize-giving in front of the whole school.

Walking up the three steps to the stage of the school auditorium, standing in the centre of the stage in front of the gold curtain, she gazes out at her schoolmates and beyond them to the gold at the auditorium windows.

She hears the principal congratulating her.

She is supposed to say thank you, but says nothing and rushes off. The principal's voice follows her, his words, the simple ones, 'Well done.'

Years later, when as a Scottish international she returned to this very auditorium for a special prize-giving, she would accept her prize with more aplomb. And much, much later, she would smile and weep and hold her arms aloft, victorious, accepting grander medals at many far grander occasions. At those moments she would feel tremendous emotion, but it is doubtful that any prize had as deep an effect on Liz Lynch as this first one.

The girl who had never been able to do anything right at school suddenly became one of the two most applauded pupils at St Saviour's. The other was the bespectacled chess champion who was making a name for himself even beyond Dundee and who is still working at becoming a grand master. He was the brains of the school, Liz was the brawn.

The pink chart on the wall at St Saviour's near the light, airy, excellent, brick-walled gym tells the story of the effect Harry's early training was having on Liz. In her first year, S1, Liz set no school records. By S2, not a year after starting with Harry, she had the 200-, the 400- and the 800-metre records.

In the training diaries which Harry taught her to keep Liz logged all their sessions and, as he had said to, her feelings on the day. Sometimes those feelings included anger aimed at Harry when he wanted her to do what she didn't want to do.

'That Harry Bennett,' she would write. 'I'm never ever going to speak to him again. Hate him, hate him.'

And the next day, 'Everything OK again.'

There were more good days, as Liz's mother Betty recalls, than bad ones when Liz, slamming the front door of the three-bedroom flat, would growl, 'I hate that Harry Bennett,' and rush into the bedroom she shared with Karen to write it down, in all its ferocity, in her training diary. By her lights, he had either worked her too hard or too lightly – no one can remember – but her feelings were fierce. Writing down everything every day, so that she and Harry could reflect back on how they were doing at the end of a year, helped keep her emotions in check.

Discipline did not come easily. Yet she stuck with it.

'And if she won a race,' Betty Lynch remembers, 'Harry was her God.'

Liz was thirteen when Harry told Phil, 'I think she's going to be really good.' He couldn't say yet how good. 'It all depends on whether she can train for another seven or eight years.'

So now there were three wise men. Kearns, her father and Harry. Each recognized that in her ability to run Liz Lynch was 'something special'. The three of them would continue to help Liz follow her star.

Even so, the odds against headstrong Elizabeth Lynch, the Whitfield girl, ever making anything of herself either as a runner or an anything else were horrendous. The older she got the tougher it would be, especially when the time came to earn a living, because even if Liz were to make a go at running there was, except for the very fortunate few, virtually no money in it. Whatever they say about Liz now, her early motivation couldn't have been money.

The fresh air, which she insists on – Liz won't allow cigarettes in her house and has bought her father, a smoker, two ionizers for his – may have been a lure to the young Liz, who ran beyond the limits of her polluted inner city into the countryside in training.

Running in the mornings before school, Liz was often late, sometimes by nearly half an hour. 'You get some who come in a lot later than that, but usually not for such a good reason,' says the school clerk Mrs Jean Tully.

Arriving at St Saviour's after the bell, Liz would present herself without a word at the entry booth. It happened quite often, but Liz explained nothing. She stood there silently in her black uniform with its striped red-orange and black tie while Mrs Tully filled out the late slip, Liz's name, class, the time she came in and signed it. Then Liz would take it to her class. After school when she wasn't working or at lunchtime after eating, Liz would visit her grandparents practically every day.

*

'Liz liked her granddad,' her father says. 'He never remembered the names of his grandchildren, he had so many, but he always knew her. "Here's me runner coming to visit me," he would say.' Liz's grandparents, her father's parents, had thirteen children. 'Beats me how we survived,' Liz's father says. His parents, who came from Sligo in Ireland, lived a five-minute run from St Saviour's.

'She would always get a sweet from her grandmother, a nice woman. She was a very holy woman, always in the church attending mass. Actually Liz is the same. Every week, never misses church, takes her wee baby with her as well, goes to St Thomas's in Arbroath. Like her grandparents, like my son-in-law too, she's a good Catholic. She's actually even got our wee kid blessing herself.'

Liz has never, to my knowledge, said a word in public about her faith. Perhaps she feels it a private matter, or perhaps no one has yet asked her. Many of sport's great champions are religious. Carl Lewis, Chris Akabusi, to name two great runners, and Freddie Spencer, the former grand prix world motorcycle racing champion, are born-again Christians. The American marathoner Joan Benoit has written in her autobiography of her deep faith.

Track sessions with Harry were twice weekly, on Tuesdays and Thursdays after school, and often at weekends too. Liz pushed herself so hard whenever she ran that her posture soon deteriorated and by mid-session she would be terribly stooped. Harry Bennett called it 'the athletic slouch' and he lessened it, but he couldn't get rid of it in Liz because she had a particularly long and often sore back and pushed herself hard. Finishing the session exhausted, she'd put her hands on her hips and lean forward, gasping air, too tired to hold up that long back even a second more.

Once Liz started running she was hard to stop. If five miles were good for her, she thought ten would be better. She was like many runners are: addicted. Running gives you a natural and healthy biochemical high. Because she was often already tired when she arrived at the track, Harry had sometimes to curtail training.

'Harry was not able to do all of the speed work with her he had planned,' says Barbara Oliver.

Harry sometimes complained about this to his running companions, Barbara's husband Ron Oliver, a useful club runner, and Phil Kearns who still jogged that half-hour a day. Harry also ran at lunchtimes on his own. But even if he spoke to her about it, it is doubtful Liz ever got the message.

Harry had a theory that you ought to develop speed as quickly as you could, because speed-building was like learning a language – easier the younger you were.

'Any speed you have,' Harry told his running mates Kearns and Oliver (who is now also a teacher), 'you have when you're young.'

Enough was going right, however, to convince Harry: 'I don't yet know if she has it in her to be world class, but the lassie is going to be champion of Scotland.'

Liz was still a holy terror.

On the bus to races Gail Pope, the club cross-country captain, had her work cut out keeping Liz Lynch under control. Liz was so full of energy, so hyper, it was contagious and no matter what threats were made by any captain or monitor, there at the back of the bus would always be Liz laughing and jumping about in high spirits.

Liz didn't so much flout discipline as go her own way. 'I've always been headstrong,' she concedes.

Try as she might, Gail couldn't do very much about it. Liz wanted to do what Liz wanted to do. This tug of wills between the responsible older girl and the spirited younger one would eventually lead to a beautiful friendship. They would see each other only on training nights, but during the four years that they were together in Harry's training group Liz came to look on Gail Pope as a kind of big sister, one she could 'yap and chat with' about the last training session or the next race, or problems with Harry.

By this time Gail was working in a bank. Liz was sixteen, had left school and had a job in W. H. Scott's jute factory 'weaving, putting spools on machines, it was pretty boring, and there was a lot of oil and dirt'. Liz's lungs were craving countryside air.

The work was part of a youth training scheme for which she was paid weekly 'mere sweeties' of £23.50. Worse, she wasn't really needed there. If she had wanted to, Liz will tell you, she could have spent the whole year at the factory sitting on her bum scoffing cream buns all day.

At least when she'd worked after school till late in Andrew Smiley's fish and chip shop, Smiley had noticed she was there and driven her home at night. Smiley's Strathmore Fish Bar, where Liz wrapped her cod and chips carryout first in greaseproof paper and then newspaper, was not in the best part of town.

Picking berries at the fruit farm, or picking potatoes, had been her occupations in the school holidays. It was tiring physically, but Liz had plenty of energy and the focus of her life was already on her training.

At the factory, she had to clock in at five-thirty a.m. but Liz devoted her evenings and weekends to running. 'Everyone thought it was so weird, because girls are only supposed to be bothered about boys, discos and Babychams. I never had a boyfriend for longer than a week because they couldn't understand what I was doing.'

If it had flickered through her mind, she had never seriously thought of running as an escape route. Now she began to hope it would take her out of Whitfield. 'When I was sixteen I did; when I was thirteen, fourteen, no, I just loved running.'

For a long time she'd known she needed to run. 'That's been my life since I was eleven. I've always needed to run and other things must not interfere. I'm very headstrong and if I want to do something I go out and do it.'

It was already instinctive to make sure nothing interfered, to work other things around running, even though Liz wasn't actually winning a great many races. Instead, heart-breakingly, she was coming second or third, often behind a blonde-haired wisp of a girl called Yvonne Murray, of whom we would all be hearing much more later.

The problem was that the races were too short. Liz lacked the sprint finish of the others but could keep running fast for what seemed like for ever. She had enough basic speed and stride length to enable her sometimes to win shorter races, but she didn't have much of a sprint and fell back when the others upped the pace and kicked past her at the end of the race. The gist of her talent was her stamina, her innate ability to keep going.

'The longer the distance,' Liz would realize fairly early, 'the more naturally I can run – I feel comfortable, I don't feel that I have to put the work in that some of the other girls do.'

Even when she was sixteen Harry used to say, 'The ten thousand is your event.' It would be ten years before Harry was proved right.

At the time, the longest distance girls and women typically ran was a mile. Not quite double that, the 3000 metres had just come on to the track horizon, but it was thought long distances like the 10,000 metres and the marathon were too tough for women.

'One day, Liz,' Harry soothingly predicted to his miserable protégée, 'that attitude will change, and you will run the ten thousand metres at the Olympics.'

Liz certainly liked the idea of it.

Gazing thoughtfully at a point somewhere beyond her, Harry quickly calculated the years of training she would need, multiplying that by the lumbering speed of sporting politics. Then he predicted that in the 1990s she would run for Britain at a major championship and the 10,000 metres would be hers.

'I told him he must be off his head.'

It was an uncanny, extravagant prediction, characteristic of Harry's generous nature, and highly unlikely to come true with attitudes as they were then, for the women's 10,000, the very distance at which Liz would eventually win the world championship, was not even a gleam in the most radical athletic official's eye.

But coach and athlete enjoyed the moment, as they enjoyed many a moment, although between Liz and Harry it was not always sweetness and light.

— 3 —

A Leg Up

One evening en route to the chippie on the posher side of town, where they usually gorged on plaice and chips on Tuesday and Thursday nights immediately before training, Liz confided to Gail Pope that Harry was 'in a mood' with her.

Harry would get in a mood with you if he thought you were letting yourself down. Harry didn't argue with you. If he wasn't happy about something he just wouldn't speak to you.

'He would go into a mood and basically ignore you for a couple of weeks,' Gail Pope says. 'You would do the training and that, he would tell you what training to do, but you would know he wasn't very happy with you because he would make it clear his mind was on something or on someone else.' You would sense the icy emotional temperature and feel frozen out. But Harry always did it for a reason.

Harry must think I can run a heck of a lot better than I am doing, Liz mused, or he wouldn't be in a mood with me. She was going through a bad patch in her running.

'I'm really fed up at the moment,' she told Gail. 'I come second and third all the time. Ach, I never seem to be winning anything.'

Liz had taken it almost in her stride when taller, four-months-younger Yvonne Murray, who would be her perennial rival, beat her down to silver at the Scottish Schools Cross-country Championships, a one-and-a-half-mile race. Yvonne, whose mother like Liz's was a barmaid, though only part-time, would develop into Britain's prime champion at middle distance, at which she would always be faster than Liz. But at 10,000 metres Liz would be pre-eminent.

Yvonne Murray, who would win the European 3000-metre

championship in 1990, still lives in Musselburgh, near Edinburgh. Christine Haskett, who was a dozen years older, was an entirely different issue. She had been Harry's first star and had moved down to England. When she turned up and beat Liz at the Scottish Championships Liz wept bitter tears. What right, she had angrily asked all and sundry, did an Anglo-Scot have to Scottish titles?

What it all added up to was that Liz was losing, even if, as Harry was always telling her, the races which were open to girls and women were too short to show off her talents. Feeling miserable, Liz didn't know what she should do.

'What if you worked harder at it?' Gail asked, the conversation continuing as they ate. 'Because that's what Linsey Macdonald's doing.' Linsey Macdonald was an Olympic bronze medallist. Few girls could ever hope to beat her.

Liz munched a chip thoughtfully. She was already running thirty or so miles a week, a lot for a teenage girl. They left the chippie, not Smiley's but the Ferry Fry-In which was posher with fancy lighting and plastic-topped tables, for their regular rendez-vous with Barbara Oliver, who was Harry's right-hand woman at the track and always gave them a lift in her car to Caird Park. Training with the group was from seven p.m. until nine or nine-thirty.

Everything seemed to be as usual except that Liz had made a decision. Without another word to Gail, or a single word to Barbara, Liz upped her mileage. Running alone, she went to forty miles a week, fifty, an unheard-of sixty. Seventy. She just kept piling on the miles.

'I'm running over sixty miles a week,' she confessed. She was now pounding out four, maybe five million strides a year, each stride requiring some thirty muscles to cooperate. Didn't it hurt her knees, ankles, Achilles tendon, feet, shins, calves? The answer then as now was no: 'The tough training programme is no problem.' Her body seems to be cast of iron.

Even years later Liz has never been seriously injured by that pounding, although she has been sore. Once, when she ran into something, she did crack a bone in her knee. 'I feel really silly about that. It happened when I tripped over a tree stump in Caird Park.'

Instead of taking a year off as one doctor suggested, Liz wore a flexible knee brace and kept training. Of course, now that she is a one-woman business with an annual turnover in a vintage year in the vicinity of half a million dollars – though she has never admitted to it – Liz believes in an ounce of prevention for those long, stove-pipe legs. 'Och, aye, you've got to take care. In Florida there's a masseur who has taught my husband Peter how to rub my legs with baby oil every day after training.'

Not all champions enjoy training. Liz has always loved it, the tougher the better. In the wintertime Harry would send Liz and the others in her training group out on hill sessions, Dundee having quite long steep braes. Bundled into several thicknesses of track suit, Liz would run up Caird Avenue to Klepington Road, all the way to the Kingsway and then up another hill, doing a circuit where Harry had somehow arranged it so that every hill went upwards. When Liz felt herself beginning to flag, Harry, perched on the top of the hill, would shout down to her, 'Come on, lassie. You can do it. Rely on your superior strength.'

And Liz would realize anew that she did have superior strength. Harry had a way with people, and could get the best out of them no matter how hard they had to work. He had a certain charisma, making Liz want to run really well not just for herself but to please him. Harry believed she could do it, and that spilled over making her believe she could do it herself.

In the summer season there were 'killer sessions' on the track. Liz and the four or five other girls in the group would warm up by jogging for two or three laps; then some stretches; then a murderous set of 600 metres, with brief recoveries, three times, flat out.

Or Harry would set them six fast laps of the 400-metre track, with the usual 90-second recovery jog between each lap. This set taught speed and racecraft, too, because it was impossible at this distance to sprint the whole time.

The dagger through the heart would be a 200-metre run followed by a 300-metre run followed by a lap of the 400-metre track followed by a 600-metre run, with quite short recovery periods between each one.

Apart from the group training, Liz was working with Harry on Saturdays and some Sundays if they weren't racing. This hard work culminated before her seventeenth birthday in what Liz had so craved: the honour of representing Scotland. But that first junior international at Gateshead left an unexpectedly sour taste in her mouth.

The journey south to the north-east of England, 'my first international trip', unfortunately 'was quite a hassle'. The hassle had less to do with the motorway than with the mind.

There was, she recalls, 'just a wee problem' about the team kit. Not only was there no generous 'expenses' money going round, there was no free kit. Liz was lent a Scottish team track suit and some Addidas shoes to wear at Gateshead.

'But to keep them, you had to pay fifteen pounds for the track suit and I think it was twenty pounds for the shoes. So after the meeting I had to give them all back.'

With her ulcer-ridden father Martin one of the long-term unemployed and her mum working as a barmaid it had been hard enough finding the fifteen pounds Liz needed to pay towards her travel costs. Posh luxuries like a squad track suit, no matter how much she wanted them, were out.

It hurt. To this day, says Barbara Oliver, Scottish internationals are only lent their kit. It must cause many problems. Liz never forgot. Rising expectations, historians tell us, lead to revolution. The totally down-trodden are too frail to rebel. Liz had always been a strong character.

When Liz Lynch outraced Scotland's Olympic bronze medallist Linsey Macdonald in the English Open Championship *and* in the Five Nations Cup, in 1981, the local *People's Journal* shouted, 'Liz Has Beaten Olympic Star'. It should have said, 'twice'.

At just eighteen, Liz had had the honour of representing Scotland sixteen times, counting from school level upward, and was being featured in the local papers. Unemployed, she was now a full-time athlete, living on the dole and signing on. The famous British champions who have lived on benefit are legion, far too numerous to count. One day when the plaudits are awarded someone should hand a trophy to the DHSS.

With more time to give to it, Liz's training became increasingly intense. She was doing a murderous amount of mileage: 'I do a lot of road running, about eighty miles a week in winter. Harry Bennett accompanies me on a motorbike.' Harry had never owned a car. He loved motorbikes, but in the old days, when he was fitter and the mileage was lower, he used frequently to accompany his athletes on foot.

'Harry was working the poor girl so hard,' Vi Bennett recalls, 'that I thought there had to be a good reason. I knew Harry knew what he was doing, so I never asked him.'

But her husband sensed that she needed an answer: 'If Liz comes through this out the other end, there ain't nobody'll beat her, Vi,' Harry said. 'Nobody.'

Instead of alcohol, which the other girls drank, Liz liked passion fruit juice after races when the whole club would go to the pub in Victoria Road. She had style. If there was no passion fruit she drank orange juice. She had tasted cider, but didn't like it much.

The others wore lots of eye make-up, not Liz. But she was interested in clothes, then as now. 'She was always very, very smart and up-to-date with all the fashions,' one of the other girls in the group recalls, 'wearing bright colours and those short trousers and really smart jackets that were current then. Even on her low budget Liz was able to look good.' There was not that much talk in the pub about things like John Lennon's murder or the war in the Falklands. Running was a big subject – and, for most of the girls, boys. For Liz, however, boys were not a major preoccupation.

Girls growing up in a place like Whitfield are always warned of the dangers of liking boys too much. Stay away from boys is the message, or you'll be another one caught in the trap.

'When I see the faces of the girls pushing a pram along the street with two wee ones hanging on,' Liz would say, 'I know that just couldn't be me.'

Everyone else would stay late at the pub, but Liz had to be up early to run.

'All roads lead to Rome,' they say, but in Liz's case the high road turned out to be *from* Rome. There in the 1982 World Junior

Cross-country Championships Liz finished a dehydrated fifty-seventh or so, which was good enough to catch the eye of a wise scout from a small American college who asked Liz if she would be interested in going west to seek her fortune.

Liz's initial reaction was adamant: 'No way.'

And that was that, until the evening of the winter solstice. 'A phone call at five-thirty p.m. on 21 December 1982 was the major turning point of my athletic career.'

The transatlantic conversation was brief. Just as she had told the other man, Liz said, fairly sharpish, 'No.'

'Who was that?' her father asked.

'He was calling from America. He wants me to go over there to college on a sports scholarship.'

'You don't know anyone in America,' Martin Lynch said.

'Aye.'

But people in America knew of her. Bob Wood, a recruiting officer for Ricks, a junior college in Idaho, had been looking through the 1982 Great Britain junior ranking lists and saw her name. 'At that time I was third in the three thousand metres.' Bob Wood rang her three nights in a row, offering a full scholarship to Ricks. 'All I needed was a one-way air ticket.'

However, the answer, vehemently uttered, was still no 'because I had never been away from home before' – except very briefly for athletics meetings. 'The thought of leaving scared me and I loved my family too much.'

Unwilling to take no for answer, Bob Wood rang Harry.

Martin Lynch was unaccustomed to seeing Harry at Inveresk Crescent. But Harry had come over to Whitfield, trudged up the filthy stairs, walked along the graffiti-scarred passage and was now sitting on the sofa in Martin Lynch's comfortable lounge. 'But what is there for Liz here, Martin?' he was saying. 'If she gets her chance, one day she will be one of the greatest athletes the world has ever seen.'

Martin was stunned at Harry prophesying that.

'She's the best athlete ever come through my hands, Martin.'

Again Martin was astounded. Harry had coached plenty of Scottish internationals. 'But Elizabeth knows no one in America.'

'If athletics can give the lassie an opportunity to see the world, and she will get an education, why shouldn't she use it?'

'My daughter is not interested in studies.'

'The course is in PE, which will suit Liz.'

'She's refused flatly and we are nae keen for her to go. She is just a young girl. All my kids have been kept pretty close to home.'

Harry persisted. 'What future is there for her here?' he asked. 'What qualifications does she have?'

None to speak of.

In recalling that day Martin says, 'We had a good talk. He convinced us. Harry had an answer for everything, and though we were not certain how we would raise the necessary money for the air ticket and that, he convinced me and her mother that this would be the best opportunity for Elizabeth in the circumstances. "Harry," I said, "I'll speak to my daughter."'

In the face of this concern and lobbying, Liz still felt doubts. What appealed to her about the offer was that travelling to races would stop costing her money. 'In America all your expenses are paid by the college. They also arrange top-class coaching for their students and special races against other good runners.'

If she did go to America at the end of February for the new semester she would be thrown in at the deep end, smack into the indoor season. She went to Harry, Vi Bennett clearly remembers, and asked, 'What should I do?'

Harry repeated what he had said to Martin: 'What opportunity is there for you here, Liz?'

'It was a big heave leaving my parents, but I knew I would be able to apply myself to the running side of things because I am very dedicated to training and determined to get the most out of myself.'

'After talking it over with me, my dad was determined to raise enough money for a ticket.' At that time she and her father were both unemployed and the family had no extra money. It was estimated that it would take a frightening £1200 to cover the return air fares, new clothes and necessary sundries.

'A raffle was set up,' Liz recalls. 'A few local companies were approached and some of my relatives also helped out, as did Harry.'

Harry's wife Vi knew Harry had given a personal donation, but he never told her it was one hundred pounds, a great deal of money to them at the time. Liz's Uncle Alec, a roadworks foreman, gave a large chunk of his savings. Alec Wilson, who was actually her mother's uncle and therefore a great-uncle, was always very generous.

At the Dundee Hawkhill Harriers club house a jumble sale was announced with every penny of the proceeds to go to Liz.

At nine-thirty p.m. on the last day of 1982 Liz's sister Karen was ironing the clothes for that night's Hogmanay celebratory perambulations. 'If you're a Scot, at Hogmanay,' Karen will tell you, 'you house tidy, spring clean, make lovely food and dress up and have people over.'

Martin Lynch had gone to fetch Betty from the pub early because this year they were having the family over. Everyone called on everyone into the wee hours. Liz and some of the other girls Harry coached were going to turn up at the Bennetts' late, as they did every Hogmanay, knowing Vi would dish up a plate of steak pie and peas for each of them.

Karen, who didn't mind a spot of ironing, suddenly slammed the iron down on the ironing board. Pain shot up her right shoulder and into her neck. She felt alarmingly hot, sweaty and very frightened as the pain seared her right arm and then turned it numb. 'I have these terrible pains, I feel horrible,' she gasped, putting her face against the cool glass of the kitchen table.

Liz and her brother Kevin were terrified. Their sister was twenty and a half years old; you don't have heart attacks before you're twenty-one, do you? Either her brother or Liz phoned their parents at the pub. They hurried home and, taking one look at Karen, rushed her to Ninewells Hospital.

It wasn't a heart attack, but it was serious. Karen's lung had collapsed. 'That was the first time the lung collapsed,' Martin Lynch remembers. 'Unfortunately, we had had blood trouble with Karen when she was an infant, all kinds of bother. Karen was weakly.'

God had parcelled out all the potential for physical strength in the female side of the Lynch family to Liz. She had been an unusually lucky little girl. A rich little poor girl. Although he had sons, her father had let her in on sport and Phil Kearns and Harry had long since convinced Liz that running was what made her special.

Going off to America was her best shot at the future, and it would be a crying shame if she let them and herself down by turning her back on her destiny. She could be a champion. She was the strong one.

That's why, despite her fears, she was going. 'The hardest part was saying goodbye to my family and Harry.' It was a horrible, heavy day with 'pocketing' rain. 'When I boarded the bus to London the reality of what I was about to do just hit me. I sat crying for the entire journey because I suddenly felt very alone and scared.'

Her father certainly shared her trepidation. Martin waved and waved to her, his youngest, until the bus pulled out of the station and she began her journey to America, a wee lass of eighteen knowing nobody when she got there, not a soul.

— 4 —

My Own Private Idaho

Idaho was a shock. The climate was ice or fire.

What was all that rubbish about the streets of America being paved with gold? In Rexburg, Idaho, they were often paved a foot deep in snow. Ricks College was in the heart of the Rocky Mountains, where the temperature can be twenty degrees below zero Fahrenheit for weeks on end. In the last dark days of February, mid-winter, Liz stepped off the plane into sub-zero weather that made Scotland seem like the tropics.

Even a girl hurrying to her classes paused before going out to smoothe a thick, sticky coating of Vaseline over her chapped lips and cheeks. Sometimes at night the thermometer fell to minus thirty-eight Fahrenheit. The icicle stalactites hanging from the window frames pierced young Liz's heart.

Even odder, when summer came, the daytime temperature could reach ninety. Sprinklers kept the college lawns green as an oasis in what would otherwise be a high desert: arid, barren, burnt out. The location of Rexburg in the west of the American continent made it subject to these terrible extremes of weather. As if inspired by the climate, the college rules and regulations were extreme.

So much was forbidden in Idaho.

Ricks was a Mormon college and their religion ruled out coffee and tea, which were regarded as stimulants. Chocolate was banned, too. Soon Betty was sending off lumpy packages of Mars bars and tea bags very thoroughly wrapped so no one at the school would realize that the parcel from across the sea contained these bootleg items.

When Liz rang home or they rang her (they alternated every

fortnight) Martin and Betty held their youngest's hand across the wire. 'For the first six weeks I was very homesick and used to get upset when my parents phoned.'

She finally settled in. 'I shared with three other girls. One was Irish, which helped me a lot.'

But there was so much to get used to there where even the air was different, thinner than British air because of the high altitude. Rexburg, Idaho, is at 5000 feet. The highest point in the British Isles, Ben Nevis, is 4406 feet. This aspect of the strange foreign geography was actually a tremendous piece of luck.

Ever since the 1968 Olympics in Mexico City, which is at 7200 feet, it had been recognized that training at altitude could be a great boon to athletes. Sprinters and jumpers could vastly improve their performances because the natural air pressure is reduced. But the air, which has less oxygen than does air at sea level, makes running longer distances harder and slower – until your body acclimatizes. Then you can find yourself well ahead of the opposition. The secret weapon of the Kenyans, who are coming to dominate middle and longer distances in athletics, is the fact that their country is situated at altitude.

But the altitude of Rexburg was not at the forefront of young Liz Lynch's mind as she struggled to settle down in Mormon country. As well as frowning on coffee, tea and junk food, the stern, closely-knit Mormon community believes in hard work, prayer and the strict Protestant ethic. Religion was important at Ricks, and of course Liz wasn't Mormon. She had been reared as a Catholic, but no one seemed to mind that she was of the wrong religion.

The Ricks students were friendly, although they all talked funny and they thought she did.

'Oh, you're English,' one girl said on hearing Liz's accent.

'I'm a Scot.'

'Isn't that the same thing?'

Ricks took some adjusting to. It was a completely new world. Beyond that, there were the demands of her studies and the demands of her racing schedule, and there was the acute problem of money. The other students seemed to have so much more of it. The Americans drove big cars through their big Western spaces.

The children of the rich, it is said, never expect anything bad to happen to them. The children of the poor are more likely – because they have more reason – to have chips on their shoulders.

It was probably at Ricks that not having enough money began to really bother Liz.

She had been given what the Americans refer to as a 'full ride'. Her scholarship supposedly covered everything: her tuition was paid for, so was her room and board. But there was no provision for clothes or special things to eat or even toothpaste. Scholarships don't take into account that sort of thing.

Liz had always liked nice clothes. And at her age clothes are regarded as particularly important. It was not easy to be less well dressed than she wanted to be, less done up than so many of the others. And she had to remind herself to think first before she bought absolutely anything.

The chronic lack of money in Dundee had been her parents' problem. Liz had always had to make a contribution with what she earned from the job at Smiley's when she was still at school, from the sojourn in the jute factory, and even from her dole money. But she was usually able to save up to buy what she wanted. Keeping things going at home had never been her responsibility. And when she needed extras, her parents and Harry or someone in the family like Uncle Alec had always managed to find the money. In Idaho, Liz was on her own.

For the first time there was no one to intervene on her behalf because she was special. The responsibility for keeping herself had abruptly landed on her own shoulders. Suddenly, Liz was her own breadwinner. She had to grow up.

Like every other mortal, from time to time, Liz now felt the unfairness of life. At times she was resentful at having less than the other students, and more than a little frightened knowing that it was down to her. The frustration of having to think about what others took for granted would have made anyone stew.

Liz being Liz, however, didn't just stew. She did something about it. Working your way through college is an old American tradition, since there are no automatic student grants. Some of the country's greatest statesmen and businessmen – and businesswomen – tell stories of the odd jobs they took to put themselves through college or university.

Liz felt she had a knack for hair cutting. She had sometimes cut her own. So in Idaho the girl whose hair wouldn't do anything that she told it to became the dormitory's unofficial hairdresser.

Her fee was a dollar, two dollars, three dollars a head. Business was brisk.

Track, the reason she was here, was going so-so. It wasn't that she wasn't winning. Triumph followed upon triumph, starting with double gold in her American track debut only weeks after her arrival. The runners at the Idaho State Invitational, who had been astonished at the unknown new girl's romp to victory in both the 800 and the 1500 metres, soon learned to be worried whenever they saw Elizabeth Lynch's name on the programme.

Liz's problem was not her own racing, but their coaching methods.

She wrote to Harry sending copies of the ridiculous training schedules given her by her new coaches, and was surprised when Harry wrote back and told her to follow them. The letters between them kept flying across the Atlantic.

There were so many things she didn't like about the coach or the college. She didn't like them tinkering with her training, which she and Harry had got pretty right. The Americans have a saying, 'If something ain't broke, don't fix it.' Nonetheless, they kept meddling.

To be honest, sometimes Liz liked it at Ricks and sometimes she felt the place was fairly horrible. So far away from home, in the midst of strangers, she couldn't help feeling alone.

Then she met another scholarship student, a runner, male.

'It definitely wasn't love at first sight. In fact we didn't much like each other.' But as soon as she set eyes on Peter McColgan Liz must have been somewhat interested. Blue-eyed, black-haired, handsome, long-legged like herself, Peter was from Northern Ireland. Liz's grandfather had come from Ireland.

Peter was a steeplechaser. He came from Strabane, but to the Americans they were both more-or-less English.

Liz first noticed him one morning at the track, and thought him unfriendly.

She didn't make a very good first impression on Peter, either. He thought she was stroppy: 'The first time I met her, I went up to the track. There was some girl there shouting at the coach. She was tearing him apart in front of everybody. This girl thought something was wrong with the training and she wouldn't shut up about it. I noticed her all right.'

Peter is soft-spoken and slow to voice any anger. To this day, he tends to go quiet when angry; Liz bursts out. What he witnessed that day convinced him she was contrary.

Then the Ricks team went to the US Junior College Cross-country Championships in Texas. Watching in amazement as this Liz Lynch 'buried everybody', Peter thought, she is really something.

What she had been doing in that public argument at the track, he now decided, was standing up for herself.

They were opposites, and opposites attract. Peter's own attainments were and always had been, like his manner, relatively modest. His early athletics career, it amused him to note, was something of a catalogue of disaster. He had been a late bloomer, competing in athletics at grammar school in Omagh, but definitely more interested in football – and his track results showed it.

He became a tax officer after leaving school. At the Inland Revenue Athletics Championships at Crystal Palace, his first big steeplechase meeting, 'Everything went wrong for me during the race. I had difficulty with the water jump, fell four or five times, and finished well down the field. It was devastating, and I made up my mind not to run in the steeplechase again.'

He was lured out of thoughts of early retirement by what seemed a good chance to make a Northern Ireland team that was going abroad to compete.

He finished second in the team trials, 'and as there was only one place, I didn't go on the trip.' However, his time of 9 minutes, 11 seconds, third fastest in his age group that year, put him in the top ten British juniors. Inspired, he won a place on the Northern Ireland under-20s team.

Like Liz, Peter got a call from America pretty much out of the blue offering him a scholarship. 'I had been working in the tax office for several years, and welcomed the chance. I went to Ricks College, and it was there I met Liz.'

A year older than Liz, who had started in the spring term at the end of February 1983, Peter McColgan arrived at the college six months later in September. And before long he found that what he liked most about America was Liz.

He wooed her with red roses. She was, he soon found out, already dating someone, 'a balding Mormon who said he was from Texas money and studying to be a doctor'. If not for Peter, the family joke goes, Liz would have been richer sooner, a cattle millionaire.

When the college closed for the Thanksgiving or Easter holidays, foreign students were allowed to stay on as it would cost them hundreds to fly home. Very often Ricks provided paying work, odd jobs around the place that needed doing, so that the students could profit from the holiday.

It was over one of these holiday periods, while Liz was earning money washing windows and Peter was cleaning out flats, that they got to know each other better.

Their first date, Peter recently recalled, was at a ten-pin bowling alley.

'Not at all,' Liz countered. 'I remember that the very first time we went out it was to a bar though neither of us are drinkers. We two runners were among the very few non-Mormons in college, we had to do something to get away.'

In love, they soon became an item. They saw a lot of each other and not just at the track, and they went off to competitions together with the team. Romance suited them both. They were very happy.

Sometimes the college seemed almost more interested in converting Liz to Mormonism than on capitalizing on her talent. Neither Liz nor Peter was interested in converting, nor had this been a factor in their getting scholarships. But like Bob Wood, the Ricks recruiting officer, there were religion boosters there who wouldn't take no for an answer. Long after she left the college, proselytizers in search of a convert would find their way to her home in Britain and knock on the door. Liz would usually be away somewhere running, and it often fell to her father to point out that his daughter was satisfied with the religion she already had.

Americans work hard and play hard. At Ricks they kept their runners busy. And expected them to deliver. In competition, Peter was doing fairly well, but Liz was making a name for herself. Starting with that debut victory, she set the 1983 season on fire.

A few days before her nineteenth birthday she achieved a new American championship record of 9 minutes 39 seconds in the 3000 at the National Junior College Championships in San Angelo, Texas, and came second in both the 800- and the 1500-metre races. Then, at a meeting in Oregon, she set championship records and took triple gold, in the 3000, 1500 and 800 events, and silver in the team relay. She was still pushing herself hard. Her times, much lower than her personal bests, were phenomenally good since the meeting took place at altitude.

The 1984 season was also vintage. As the American Junior cross-country champion, Liz went with the Ricks team all the way to Arkansas for the National Junior College Indoor Championships where she took double gold, in the mile and in the two-mile events.

'That's why we decided to recruit her,' says John Mitchell, who was then the coach of the University of Alabama track team. 'I offered her a scholarship. You look at an athlete's results, and if you like what you see, you take the next step. We called her at the junior college and sent her a questionnaire.'

It was plain to Liz that Alabama had a lot of plusses. There would be better coaching, better facilities and a better grade of competition against America's finest runners. And at the end of it there was a fully fledged university degree. Ricks was a two-year college. The University of Alabama offered the standard American four-year degree programmes. Hers, in sports management, was to be undertaken over a period of five years. 'Yes,' she ticked on the questionnaire, she would consider transferring to Alabama.

'Then,' remembers Coach Mitchell, 'there were letters and telephone calls. That is normal procedure. She came down for a visit to look at the campus. We wanted to meet her personally, spend some time with her. We would do that with everybody.'

On her first visit to the American South, Liz liked what she saw, particularly the sun. The get-to-know-you visit went like clockwork. Alabama liked Liz, and Liz liked Alabama. The climate was so good you could probably train year-round. And the scholarship they were offering was for a 'full ride'.

Everybody liked everybody. Everything was ready to go and Liz was on the brink of accepting their offer to transfer to the university. The one drawback was that leaving Ricks meant leaving Peter.

Coach Mitchell was somewhat taken aback when Liz told him about her boyfriend, a brilliant steeplechaser. She would, she said, like to come to Alabama, but could she bring her boyfriend along?

— 5 —

A Visit to Harry

American contracts are full of 'sweeteners' – little extra benefits, perks. But a scholarship for your boyfriend too was not the typical sweetener offered in a college signing.

'Peter was borderline,' says Coach Mitchell. 'His times weren't that good, but we thought about it.' They wanted Liz badly, and about Peter Liz was adamant.

Liz was pleased when, after thinking hard, Alabama, in the person of Coach Mitchell, said yes. 'We had no idea,' Mitchell says, 'of what a bargain we were about to gain in Peter.'

Now, as Liz prepared to depart for Alabama, she wondered what Harry would think of John Mitchell. Her new American coach was a burly man in his forties, broader and taller than Harry. She had more confidence in him than the coaches at Ricks, but she still missed Harry.

It had been wonderful to see him on her first visit home from Ricks, a year ago. In Dundee for the summer holidays almost the first thing she had wanted to do was to see Harry. It had been like old times. No, it hadn't. Things were different, of course, but in the most important way they were the same. As coach and athlete they still clicked. Seeing Harry in his baseball cap after the months away made Liz smile.

She had learned a lot, grown up a lot since leaving, and Harry didn't try to turn the clock back. Harry never tried to hang on to his old girls. He sent them off to soar. He'd sent her off, as he had Christine Haskett, and in the few months she had then been away Liz was indeed beginning to soar.

He was coaching her again that summer of 1983, and they had a training schedule she could entirely see the point of. There were no arguments with this coach. She enjoyed Harry putting her through her paces on the Caird Park track. Sometimes there were long sessions. It was early July, and didn't get dark till late.

He even arranged a few races for her, usually on a Sunday.

That Sunday afternoon Harry was taking her to race in Fife.

In the morning Liz did her training, and Harry did his. For years Harry had been trying to get his wife Vi to go jogging with him, and he had finally persuaded her.

They went out to Finlaughen Park, which was just along from their house, and the pace was slow on account of Vi, who had only been running with him for a few weeks.

As they arrived back, jogging at a snail's pace really, Vi stopped and chatted to a neighbour. Harry, knowing she could be quite a talker, carried on into the house.

'Harry has been trying to get me to do this for my health for ages,' Vi told the neighbour. 'I'm hoping it will take the pounds off. Now that I've started, I'm finding I like it. I intend to keep it up. Harry's pleased.'

Vi and the neighbour chatted for ages, and when she went in to put on the kettle Harry was just lying there. He had probably had the pain again when they were out jogging in the park and run all the way home without a word to her about it. She rang for an ambulance.

Vi had no clear idea of exactly when it had first started, but she knew that for some time now Harry had had a touch of angina. She had no idea if it had been troubling him recently. 'Harry was a person who didnae tell you things like that. If he had a pain you wouldn't know. He kept it to himself. He told me the angina was very slight, and that the doctor had said carry on running.'

Harry's workmates at D. C. Thomson knew better because he jogged every single lunch hour for six miles and they used to look out of the factory window and see him coming back, sometimes clutching his left arm or shoulder.

At Caird Park, Barbara Oliver learned of his condition one day when she arrived early at the track and saw Harry with a stopwatch. Clutching his arm, but happy, he said with some satisfaction, 'I was able to go longer before the pain caught up with me today.'

He was playing Russian roulette.

Running was his hobby. It never occurred to him to stop. He had started in the RAF, won the Scottish 800-metre title and kept on running. For years he was a serious club runner and he also played a lot of golf. Two years earlier, when he had taken some of his girl runners in for a fitness check, it was Harry whose aerobic fitness scored highest – at least that was what he told Vi. Harry didn't drink, he didn't smoke and he was only fifty-one years old.

Harry was well aware of the dangers of angina. He knew he could become incapacitated. Become a cardiac cripple or die. His doctor had warned him.

Harry never mentioned it, but word spread through the Harriers that the doctors had told Harry he was to stop running because something was happening inside his heart, and like any muscle it could go.

One of their neighbours rang Inveresk Crescent. It was Martin Lynch who answered the telephone. Harry wouldn't be coming over that day to take Liz to Fife, the neighbour told him. Harry was dead.

'It was a very sad day when it happened,' Martin Lynch says. Liz was desolate. He had never seen his nineteen-year-old daughter in such a terrible state. Grief-stricken, she just sat there crying. No thought of the race that afternoon. No motivation, no energy, nothing. Harry always took her to the races. Harry arranged it. Martin didn't ever go. 'I didn't have a car or money for the fares. But I took her that day.

'I said, "Come on, Elizabeth, you're going to run that race." Liz was nae for going. She went over to her bedroom. She was crying in there. I convinced her. I said, "I think you should go to the race because Harry would have wanted you to go."'

She looked at her father for a time, and then got up and they went. It was an 800-metre race, and when they arrived Liz said, 'I'll win this thing for Harry.'

And she did.

*

Harry was cremated. At the funeral, Liz sat towards the front with some of Harry's other athletes. Next to her was Alison Johnson, who had been a year or so behind Liz at St Saviour's and who had broken some of the school running records Liz had set. They were both crying. The funeral was packed. 'A lot of youngsters,' Phil Kearns remembers. 'It was very, very sad.' He was seated a row behind Liz.

Gail Pope, Liz's old training partner, was seated further back with two other girls who had trained with Harry. Gail too, who had only recently heard he had angina, was shocked at Harry's sudden passing. Now, as she sat there, she remembered the day when Harry had met her parents, when she was first training with him and she was just a child.

He had told her parents, 'You know, I would rather die on the road out running, just like Bing Crosby would want to die on the golf course.'

As the Church of Scotland funeral service progressed, Martin Lynch, there with his wife as well as his daughter, thought of the day not that long ago when Harry had come to convince him that Elizabeth should go to America. They had had a good talk.

'And afterwards Harry had to write a letter to Ricks College, on Elizabeth's behalf, and I remembered him letting me see the letter. He actually wrote, "Scotland is losing one of the best athletes ever to leave Scotland's shores, Liz Lynch, and Scotland's loss is America's gain." It was a lovely letter. I thought, this man really thinks something of my lassie, ken. And she thought a lot of him. He was her second father, like. A good man.'

After the funeral, Liz was inconsolable. She was thinking seriously of giving up athletics.

'What's the point?' she asked Harry's widow when she went to pay her respects.

'Harry would wish you to go on,' Vi told her, but she could see Liz felt bereft. 'Lost without him. Liz was shattered as we all were, but more so Liz. That was the bottom fallen out of her world. She couldn't go on.'

An athlete without a coach is in a bad situation. And Harry was also a very dear friend. He had been her coach from the beginning. Even while she was working with the coaches at Ricks, she considered that Harry was her real coach.

'He was still coaching and encouraging me by letter. We wrote each other every week about my progress and he sent me a series of sessions which I would do in the mornings before doing sessions for my American coaches in the afternoon.'

Despite her own grief, Vi Bennett did her best to convince Liz not to quit. 'I knew Harry wanted Liz to get the best out of herself, to go as far as she could. He took her as far as he could, and knowing somebody else could take her that bit further he'd wanted her to go to America. That was the way Harry was. He would nae try and hold them back.'

Liz went home to the flat in Inveresk Crescent undecided as to what to do. For years now, as Harry had taught her to do so long ago, Liz had been recording her mileage and the details of her training in a diary, and writing down her feelings on the day.

Now she sat with a pen and paper, and her feelings about Harry exploded on to the page. It was a letter that could never be sent because it was a letter to herself and a letter to Harry.

It didn't say, 'I hate that Harry Bennett.'

In the calm that followed that storm of emotion Liz realized that in Dundee her destiny would be a job in a jute mill. 'Or more likely I'd be unemployed.' There was no one, either, to guide her running career. In Britain, especially north of the border, few female athletes got a great deal of attention paid to them. There was nothing for her there, she felt. And Harry would have wanted her to go on. She decided to return to America. It had been the right decision. She had won races and she had met Peter, and now they were going to Alabama.

— 6 —

An American Tragedy

The heat and the humidity were so high, Alabama could easily have been mistaken for Spain. Lush flowers were blossoming everywhere: magnolias, azaleas, scented jasmine and purple trailing wistaria. Liz much preferred this sultry weather to the ice and desert of the Rockies, even though on some days going for a walk on campus felt like stepping into a sauna.

The University of Alabama was in a sleepy little Southern town called Tuscaloosa, with a population of about a hundred thousand, most of them students. The standard 'uniform' was Bermudas or shorter shorts and cotton T-shirts. Liz and Peter, who liked to dress informally, fitted right in. Adjusting their ears to the Southerners' drawl posed minor problems, but at Ricks they had learned the American language and knew that the shoes they often went about in were 'sneakers' not 'trainers'. So there was no culture shock.

Despite its informality, the athletics department of the University of Alabama was big time, big business and very wide awake. State-of-the-art stadiums, arenas, weights rooms and many other costly adjuncts to excellence were laid on generously for Liz and other elite track athletes and in particular for the university's best-loved sportschildren, the football team. The huge sums being spent at Tuscaloosa on football would later be given prominent mention in the *USA Today* newspaper and in a book-length investigation called *College Sports Inc.*

But before that the women's track team scandal would be reported in the pages of the *New York Times*. Yes, later there would be those who felt Liz had become entangled in a hornets' nest, but for the present her sporting life (and Peter's) was as sweet as pecan pie.

The only obvious defect of the place from Liz's point of view as an athlete was that the countryside was fairly flat. This meant there would be less hill training here than she had been able to do in Dundee or in the Rocky Mountains, but as track was becoming more important to her than road-running this was not really a serious drawback.

'I was mainly a cross-country runner before track,' Liz reassured the young sports writer who interviewed her for the University of Alabama's student newspaper, the *Crimson-White*. 'I've now transformed myself.'

From the first smell of liniment wafting through the corridor from the changing rooms, Liz could have sensed that the future here held great things in store for her. The facilities at Alabama were tremendous and so was the coach. John Mitchell, with his soft drawl, specialized in hard training, which was exactly what Liz and Peter wanted and expected.

Coach Mitchell, however, soon found he was getting more than he had bargained for. The surprise was Peter. 'He turned out to be good. That was one that we stumbled into,' confesses Mitchell. 'It was very, very fortunate for us that we got Peter because his times were not all that good. They were OK to look at, but he improved so much. It was just amazing how much he improved.'

In the hot-house atmosphere of Alabama, Peter was blossoming. 'He ended up being an All-American,' Mitchell continues, 'and he was our inter-university conference champion and the University of Alabama record-holder. He was really something special.'

Even in their first weeks in Tuscaloosa, it was clear that coming here had been the right decision. Liz and Peter were happy in their rooms on campus, and on the track everything was going well.

At Alabama, where the coaches were acknowledged experts, Liz didn't have to waste her time arguing. And, she felt, 'the good thing was that there was lots of time to train (two to three hours a day) and that combined with warm weather led to good performances'.

Head coach John Mitchell and his team appeared to know everything about everything, including motivational psychology, which it was not at all necessary to apply in Liz's case. Perhaps that is why he was able to find a buoying moment for her father.

'Mitchell said,' Martin Lynch recalls, 'that he had never seen an athlete so dedicated, male or female, ever, and to train so hard as Liz was. He said she would be the greatest athlete ever.'

A compliment indeed from Coach Mitchell. 'I been around other kids. We had the world record holder in the hundred at Alabama, Calvin Smith. I've had a number of other Olympians and so forth.'

One of Liz's team-mates, Lillie Leatherwood, had won an Olympic gold medal in Los Angeles as part of the winning American 4 × 400 metres relay team. A couple of the other girls had also competed at the Olympics and one of them, Evelyn Adiru, an 800-metre runner from Uganda, was also the African Games champion.

'We had a great team,' is Liz's view, 'and we all got on well together. The atmosphere was great.'

Everything was going too well. There had to be a mosquito in the ointment.

It was two-thirty a.m. when Phil Kearns heard his telephone ringing. As he reached groggily for the phone, Kearns wasn't sure whether to be annoyed or frightened. His telephone wasn't in the habit of ringing in the middle of the night.

'Hi, is that Phil Kearns?' a deep voice drawled. 'This is John Mitchell. We got a problem.'

Phil Kearns sat up straight and didn't mention the hour.

Coach Mitchell gave the impression that this was his regular time for phoning. It was five hours earlier in Alabama, which wasn't operating on Greenwich Mean Time.

The trouble, as Mitchell explained in detail to Kearns, was with the university's paperwork. It concerned Liz.

Because she had been transferring from an American college to Alabama, it had been assumed that she had a high school diploma or something equivalent. Belatedly, the university clerk had noticed that there was no record of Liz's qualifications and he was making a fuss. It was entirely possible that the United States federal government, which had strict rules concerning scholarship eligibility, was standing over him. In any event, there was a big problem.

'The whole thing now hinges, Phil,' Mitchell said, 'on a piece of paper.' Without it Liz could lose not only her scholarship but her university place.

Phil Kearns promised to do whatever he could first thing in the morning and Mitchell hung up happier, giving his usual cheery sign-off, 'Have a great day.'

Phil Kearns, however, did not feel cheerful. He was facing a problem which was not going to be easy to solve. He had promised to put something in the post to Mitchell quickly, but as to what it could possibly be he had no idea.

Because the fact was Liz had no exam qualifications.

Moreover, the records of whatever she had achieved at school might not even any longer exist. As a matter of routine pupil records were destroyed after a few years to save space.

Arriving earlier than usual at St Saviour's the next morning, Kearns enlisted the help of Mrs Tully, still the St Saviour's school clerk. Liz's school records were due to be destroyed in the next week or so, they discovered. 'It was that close.'

Frantically searching the files to find *something*, Kearns came upon Liz's very unprepossessing exam board results. This was 'some bit of record of her having sat the Scottish Certificate of Education, which you sit for national awards and then go on to higher education. You usually sit six or seven. She sat only one, in maths and she failed it.

'But a bit of paper with the year on it was issued saying you sat it, with no mention of whether you passed or not.' He photo-copied this piece of paper and sent it to America. It carried the day.

Alabama's 'British girl' was certainly not lazy. Not only Alabama but the whole Southeastern Conference soon began to take note. The Southeastern Conference was the league of big, sports-mad Southern universities in which Alabama competed. The standard was very high. As Liz went with the team to Baton Rouge, Louisiana, for the 1986 Indoor Conference Championships, she knew that the fight for the title would be even fiercer than usual. Among the opposing teams Florida and Tennessee, in particular, had teeth and the reigning champions, Louisiana State University, were absolute alligators.

Even Coach Mitchell was cautious about his women's team's chances. Only in the last three weeks had he come to believe that 'individually and talent-wise, we could race them'.

That weekend, the first in March, Liz was entered not just in the mile and two-mile races, but with more team spirit than sense of self-preservation she was also running the 1000 yards *and* anchoring the relay.

It must have seemed to the opposition that her eyes were bigger than her stomach and an upset was nigh. Or maybe they thought the Crimson Tide, as the Alabama team was called, had only one runner who was fit.

Seven championship records were felled in the course of the hotly contested championships: quite a lot. Liz was involved in chopping down three. Two records were splintered when she won her mile and two-mile races. Four minutes 35.06 seconds for the mile and 9 minutes 50.85 seconds for two miles were excellent times for her age and stage. The third record fell in the team distance medley relay.

She came second in the 1000 yards, tired perhaps. Alabama won the Southeastern Conference Championship. The total team tally was 125¾ points, three quarters of a point more than second-place Louisiana. Liz herself had contributed thirty-eight points to the Crimson Tide's total score. She was the conference champion.

It was no wonder that Mitchell was to say, 'Liz was clearly the talk of the meet. We knew how good she was from workouts, but very few other people, coaches included, did.'

Alabama thought of Liz as their star miler. 'But she could do anything,' brags her coach. 'She could run anything from eight hundred up to the ten thousand, and just had a tremendous range, very, very good. She did cross-country too, the whole thing.

'When we recruited her,' Coach Mitchell continues, 'we knew

she was going to be good but we didn't know she was going to be that good. She just kept getting better and better.'

Mitchell himself was voted the conference's Coach of the Year by a ballot of his peers, and the 1986 indoor season was shaping up to be the women's track team's best ever.

The culmination of the season would be the national championships. Brimming with enthusiasm, the Tide travelled all the way to Oklahoma City, Oklahoma, for these National Collegiate Athletic Association (NGAA) Championships, which Texas were the favourites to win.

This was the top level of American track. Competing for the Georgia team was the now famous sprinter Gwen Torrence, who would later win silver at the world championships and gold at the Olympics.

Liz qualified in an unprecedented five events, the mile, 1500 metres, two mile, 3000 metres and the 1000 yards. Remember this was a national competition against America's best.

First in the mile, Liz set a new championship record of 4 minutes 37.73 seconds. It was not a personal best but better than anyone else had ever been able to achieve under the extraordinary pressure of competing at the nationals. 'I really wasn't surprised to win,' the new American national champion from across the sea was heard to remark. 'I'd been competing in the tough Southeastern Conference all season and the SEC finished in the top positions.' Gwen Torrence, also from the Southeastern conference, had finished first in her race.

Less than an hour after winning in the mile, Liz was back on the track, coming second in the 3000 metres. Her two fine performances garnered eighteen points for the Alabama team.

The Tide's Olympic champion Lillie Leatherwood and its African champion Evelyn Adiru, who were the other top scorers, won eight points each.

Again Liz was the heroine of the day, again her team was victorious. Crimson Tide were now the national champions. It was the first time in the University of Alabama's 155-year history that its track team, either male or female, had won the national title.

There was a great hullabaloo.

Liz had taken America by storm. She was named an All-
American, one of the highest honours the sport could bestow. In
the past two years she had won more than fifteen titles. Her
victory in the mile had been instrumental in Alabama's triumph,
a fact that was even acknowledged by the President of the United
States.

A letter from the White House sent to each member of the
team and signed by President Ronald Reagan praised the whole
Crimson Tide women's team. 'Nancy and I warmly commend
athletes and coaches alike for a job well done.' Alluding to
'several outstanding individual performances', the President referred specifically only to one, Liz's 'NCAA record in the mile
run'.

'You should be very proud,' said the President. Liz was.

Now carefully framed, the letter from the White House dated
25 April 1986, which still hangs in a place of honour on the wall
of Liz's trophy room in Arbroath, ends, 'You have our best wishes
for continued success. God bless you.'

Liz's head was not at all turned by this tremendous success.
'Just hard work has got me where I am,' was Liz's down-to-earth
assessment. 'Running is a lot like being married.' She and Peter,
now engaged, were planning to be married the following year.
'Marriage and running both take a great deal of effort on your
part for the venture to be a successful one. You're going to get
out of it what you put into it.'

Liz was putting in eighty-five miles a week in training. At least
that was what she publicly confessed to. Mitchell had reason to
think she was doing even more, running incredible distances at
her own volition. Eighty, ninety, a hundred miles a week. More
even.

'For a girl to get up into the hundreds, that's a lot of mileage,'
says Mitchell. 'She did do that, she can do that if she needs to.'

And even if she doesn't: 'Liz is one of those that I don't know
if she needs to do that in order to be successful. Some people
have to do that. The girl I've got now has to run high mileage in
order to be good because she doesn't have the leg speed. Liz has
good leg speed, so she could probably get away with less mileage
and be very successful. But she believes in what she's doing and

she's comfortable with what she's doing so she doesn't need to change that.'

Liz was also running road races in other parts of Alabama and throughout the South. During the previous November she had won prize money at the Sonat Vulcan Run in Birmingham, and on 8 March won some more at the Azalea Run in Mobile. On John Mitchell's advice, Liz had accepted cheques made out to an Alabama Track Club in Tuscaloosa which funnelled the prize money into a trust fund from which members of the club could withdraw money if necessary. This would turn out to be bad advice.

Next on the Crimson Tide's agenda was the outdoor track season. As the Crimson Tide hotshots prepared eagerly to go to Tallahassee, Florida, for the start of the outdoor season at the Dominoe Invitational, things were going so well that Liz predicted 'we should win outdoors also'.

Coach Mitchell was also feeling confident of a blue riband finale to the year with 'a lot of great performances'. His British girl, Mitchell believed, was so good that she was likely to become the American national champion at the outdoor championships in Indianapolis, Indiana, in June.

Then, less than a month after the letter of congratulations from the White House, the scandal broke.

It is said that the girl Liz had beaten in the Azalea Run in Mobile that March made a fuss because she was jealous, and told the authorities that Liz Lynch had accepted money for the race. Certainly this is the Lynch family's version of the story. It is the version that appeared in the Scottish newspapers at the time, and is the one that Liz's likely future co-autobiographer Doug Gillon told me in the press room at the 1992 United Kingdom Olympic Trials.

Whatever it was that precipitated the crisis, what happened once the finger was pointed is clear. Liz was in trouble and so was Mitchell.

Forced into a corner, the University of Alabama made an in-house investigation as to whether or not Liz Lynch had broken the amateur rules. Liz herself made no secret of the fact that she had been paid $3000 for the Azalea Run which was deposited, quite properly according to her local Dundee paper, in the All Striders Track Club in the form of a trust fund. The American papers called it the Alabama Track Club. But the Alabama committee decided that her acceptance of the prize money did violate university track rules.

John Mitchell immediately said he was to blame. The man who had been head coach of the Alabama track programme for seventeen years said he had misunderstood the rules.

'We thought we were doing things right. I thought she could accept money as long as the cheque wasn't made out to her,' Mitchell said in an interview with the *Birmingham News* which was reported in the *New York Times* and elsewhere in the national American press. Mitchell said he now understood that the NCAA rules barred a university athlete from accepting prize money of any kind and barred any organization represented by the athlete from receiving money on the athlete's behalf.

But the damage had been done. 'Alabama has had a spotless record, and because of my mistake the track team and the [university] have been embarrassed,' he acknowledged.

'I just blew it,' said Mitchell. 'I'm the guy who has caused the embarrassment.'

Worse than embarrassment was the fact that Liz lost her right to continue to compete in American university track. 'After a full in-house investigation stemming from Liz Lynch running in road races which have professionalized her,' said Ray Perkins, who was Alabama's athletics director and therefore Coach Mitchell's boss, 'and based on the finding of this investigation, the university is notifying the NCAA in a prepared report declaring her ineligible.'

Even if she hadn't realized she was doing so, Liz would be held responsible for having broken the rules.

'It's the runner's responsibility to know the rules,' said Mitchell. 'In Liz's case, it was my responsibility to know the rules for her. If I could go back and change things, I'd do it. But I can't.'

With all eyes on the track team, Liz, Peter and another student who received money in May for a race in Tupelo, Mississippi, returned their cheques which were made out to them personally. 'Mr Mitchell said we should hand the money right back, and I did,' Liz said at the time.

'They turned the cheques in when they got here,' said the university's sports information director. 'Our athletes knew they could not accept them, but we had to file a report and had to get a ruling.'

Because the money was given back, it was decided, no rules had been violated in Mississippi. Peter McColgan was spared the loss of his eligibility. Peter would be allowed to stay on.

But it was too late for Liz to solve her problem by returning the money accepted for the 23 November 1985 Sonat Vulcan Run or for the Azalea Run on 8 March. Her career as an American university track athlete was over. It must have seemed very unfair to Liz, who had done nothing no one else had done. Except get caught.

All over the world officials either turned a blind eye to what was going on, or helped launder the money. The world of athletics which Liz had entered so innocently was increasingly cynical, living a lie. Runners were pretending to uphold the old ideal of amateurism while secretly taking payments for their efforts.

The amateur rules that had been designed for well-heeled gentlemen who were part-timers at sport were impossible to uphold in a sport of full-time athletes who needed to earn a living. Instead of sensibly changing the regulations, the die-hards of sport had made petty crooks of all the athletes. They weren't amateurs, they were 'shamateurs'.

Sebastian Coe remembers the brown envelopes handed to athletes on this side of the Atlantic in the pre-trust-fund 'shamateur' days. In their book *More than A Game* Coe and his co-authors assert that 'Athletes received "expenses" worked out more for how good they were than how far they had travelled'. Payments were made in cash outside the canteen or in places like the car park. 'It wasn't a system that most of us were happy with,' Coe says. 'It forced honest people to act dishonestly – according to the strict rules then of the sport.'

As her reputation grew in America, had the amounts paid in

'expenses' to Liz grown as they had for Coe? If not, she would be one of the very few successful athletes to whom this did not happen.

'We all entered track and field with an above-the-table mentality,' a former world record holder poignantly told the BBC recently, 'and once we got into the realities of it, it became an under-the-table lifestyle.'

As far back as the 1930s, Olympic champion Mildred 'Babe' Didrikson, the greatest female athlete of her era, received illegal payments and got away with it. Others had their careers ruined.

It was in this world of sophistry that Liz had found herself. Honest and straightforward as she was known to be, she needed the money and she was no whizzkid or financier. This was the system, what else could she do but accept it?

The ad hoc and sometimes Byzantine system described by Coe worked surprisingly well because people took cash in hand for which there was no record, or cheques made out to someone else.

Actually there were lots of other scams in operation. Athletes at some universities were paid in highly saleable tickets to the big games. Some American athletes were handed credit cards belonging to people they had never heard of and told to go on a shopping spree. An athlete far from home might be given free use of a telephone line, or his mother might get a cheque. 'Golden envelopes' with large amounts of cash turned up in some athletes' lockers as if by magic. University footballers, God's chosen, even got the use of private jets and the keys to their own new cars.

Athletics was still supposedly an amateur sport, and university athletes in particular were prohibited from accepting payments, but it was common practice to accept whatever was offered.

To this day payments to athletes are made in cash, often huge amounts for which there are not always clear records, but now the table is usually set up *inside* the canteen.

Now came the crucial question. Was Liz Lynch's entire career as a runner finished, ruined because she had contravened amateur rules? If she was ineligible for American university track, wasn't she also ineligible to compete as an amateur in Britain where accepting prize money for running was prohibited? Would she be

The solemn schoolgirl in her black St Saviour's uniform. *(D. C. Thomson Ltd)*

One of the earliest running pictures. Liz, aged about thirteen, in her school kit of open-necked shirt and white shorts and what appear to be football socks.
(D. C. Thomson Ltd)

Liz never fails to remember Harry Bennett, her first coach.
(D. C. Thomson Ltd)

The job in a Dundee jute mill paid sixteen-year-old Liz £23.50 a week.
'Putting spools on machines, it was pretty boring, and there was a lot of oil
and dirt.' *(D. C. Thomson Ltd)*

The famous victory at the 1986 Commonwealth Games at Meadowbank had the whole stadium on its feet. *(Sporting Pictures)*

Above Family portrait – Liz and her parents with the new Commonwealth Games gold medal. *(D. C. Thomson Ltd)*

Below The unusual guard of honour at Liz and Peter's 1987 cathedral wedding. *(D. C. Thomson Ltd)*

Above Thousands of cheering
Dundonians welcome Liz home,
victorious after the 1990
Commonwealth Games – just as
they had after the 1986
Commonwealth Games and after
Seoul. *(D. C. Thomson Ltd)*

Left At the 1988 Seoul Olympics,
Olga Bondarenko transformed
Liz's hopes of gold to silver.
(Mike Powell/Allsport)

An athlete's calvary – with her coach John Anderson after winning Olympic silver in Seoul. *(Bob Martin/Allsport)*

Left She who laughs last laughs best. Despite appearances, in 1991 in Tokyo, Liz's greatest rival Ingrid Kristiansen lost – and Liz won the world championship. *(Associated Press)*

Below The weariness of the long-distance runner and new world champion. *(Gerard Vandystadt/ Allsport)*

deemed a professional by British officialdom? Would she never have a crack at the Commonwealth Games or at the Olympics?

This was one case in which with commendable foresight the British authorities looked after their own. In Britain a system of trust funds for athletes had recently been set up.

At the 1982 International Athletics Federation meeting in Greece, the British representative Andy Norman, who is still the most influential promoter and paymaster in British sport, had convinced the IAAF to eliminate under-the-table payments by allowing them on to the table.

That was not quite acceptable to everyone. What had been agreed instead was a kind of financial halfway house, which kept athletes officially amateurs even though they were paid for participating in sport. They could be paid appearance money for racing, but not prize money, and not directly. It had to go into trust funds which they would collect only when they retired from sport.

Had Liz received the money directly?

The answer, said the BAAB sportsman, was, if you considered carefully, no.

As the *Scotsman* reported on 28 May, 'General secretary of the British Amateur Athletics Board, Nigel Cooper, said yesterday that if Lynch had, in fact, paid her cheque into the bank – money normally never went to athletes – then it would appear she had adhered to the rules and there would be no problem.'

Where else but a bank could a cheque be paid in?

The *Scotsman* reported, furthermore, that Liz angrily denied she ran for money, and said that the cheque she received for winning the road race last March would go straight into a bank, where it would be administered in trust for her by the British Amateur Athletics Board, as was common with many top athletes.

So the day was saved. No one seems to have wondered how a cheque paid to an Alabama track club in March – and what about November? – could still exist. Had a cheque reimbursing her been issued by the club? Liz didn't really want to discuss the matter further. It no longer mattered anyway. Her ordeal was over.

The authorities in London had performed some graceful mental gymnastics. Cooper, some would say, had even gone out on a limb. The money she won, they said, would be channelled, as international rules required, into her trust fund in Britain. The only rule she had broken was the American one that no college athlete could be paid. So in American university track Liz was declared a professional; but in Britain and elsewhere, including the non-university circuit in America, she was still an amateur.

In the United States there were two sets of rules, one governing university athletics (the NCAA) and another for Olympic and inter-country competitions. The university rules dictated that athletes should not receive cash in excess of their travel and accommodation expenses. Liz had violated that rule, but accepting the prize money did not affect her amateur standing outside of the NCAA. There was no danger of her being barred from the Commonwealth Games, the World Championships or the Olympics – if she was good enough to get there.

The regulation of money in athletics remains eccentric. When Zola Budd retired and went home to South Africa, her trust fund money was handed over to her. But she has come out of retirement and is racing again as Mrs Zola Pieterse. Is anyone now asking Zola to give her money back? No.

Without the BAAB's generous backing of Liz – once again people came through for Liz Lynch when she needed it – she would never have survived as a serious runner. But it would be quite wrong to say she got off lightly. In fact, she had been the innocent victim of the cynicism and dishonesty rife in her sport.

Before the end of September Ray Perkins, who was the athletics director and the head football coach, himself would be the subject of controversy. His $120,000 salary, topped up with perks adding another $100,000 or so, would be scrutinized in *USA Today*. There would soon be questions – from outsiders – about precisely what the University of Alabama athletics department was buying when it paid out an enormous $762,000 on unspecified 'building maintenance' and another $602,200 for unspecified 'repairs/replacements'. In the 1980s, the Alabama athletics department, obviously feeling flush, went on what has been called 'a $24 million building and capital purchase spree – including $1.5 million for a private jet'. The author of *College Sports Inc.*

wonders if any of that money went to members of the football team.

Coach John Mitchell, the source of what for Liz turned out to be bad advice, was allowed to resign from the position he had held for seventeen years. 'If I could go back and change things, I'd do it,' he had said. 'But I can't. So I felt that best thing for me to do was eliminate myself from the situation.' He resigned on 24 May which coincidentally was Liz Lynch's twenty-second birthday.

Unable to get another job in coaching, he went into administration. 'I moved to Fairfax, Virginia, and was an Athletic Administrator at George Mason University for two years.' But Mitchell was a born coach. 'I missed having a team, the kids around, and I missed being around the kids and I missed the competitions,' he confesses. 'I got out of coaching and got back into it.'

In the world of American college sport, where shamateurism was the name of the game, people were quick to forgive and forget. In 1988 he returned to the Deep South as coach at the University of Georgia. He is still there.

He and Liz remain close. Every year Liz recommends three or four British athletes for scholarships. A boy from Liverpool and girl from Dundee are among those currently getting 'a full ride' at the University of Georgia largely on Liz's say-so. Mitchell hasn't forgotten how he stumbled on to Peter.

Liz landed bumped and bruised but on her feet in Scotland. The British board had saved her running life. Now Liz Lynch set about the task of letting everyone know that she was back and brilliant.

To compete in major competitions, you have to be affiliated with a club. Those are the rules. Feeling let down by Hawkhill, which gave her less support after Harry's death, she joined the St Francis Sporting Club which was known for its boxers and where she was the only runner.

She had no coach. An athlete without a coach is like a ship without a steersman at the helm, perpetually on the brink of trouble.

There is an old American saying that applies here. The other

John Mitchell, not her coach but his namesake the Attorney General under Nixon who was felled in the Watergate Scandal, was particularly fond of it: 'When the going gets tough,' that other Mitchell used to say, 'the tough get going.'

Now, Liz got going. The question was would she get anywhere?

7

Hail, Conquering Heroine

'Zola, Zola, Zola,' the South Africans had chanted when their barefoot girl runner shattered a world record in Stellenbosch Stadium and was anointed an Afrikaner heroine. Very soon after, Zola became British. While Liz's efforts in America were going unnoticed, Zola was making a name for herself in Britain, becoming a very big star. Even after bumping into Mary Decker Slaney on the track at the 1984 Los Angeles Olympics, where Zola failed to win a medal, she was still in the minds of the British authorities their finest female runner and only female star.

The authorities seemed willing to do anything for Zola. The 1986 Commonwealth Games were endangered when the African members of the Commonwealth wanted Zola out, but the British stuck by her. 'There was a lot of aggro because of Zola Budd,' Fatima Whitbread recalls. 'Although the Games were supposed to bring the Commonwealth together, this time they were tearing it apart. The Games were turning into an international catastrophe.'

Meanwhile Liz, arriving home to little fanfare, couldn't help feeling like the forgotten woman.

On 26 May, still in disgrace in America and unsure as to whether she would be allowed to return to the University of Alabama, Liz needed something to take her mind off her troubles. Fortunately she found it in Wales, at the United Kingdom National Championship where they were finally allowing women to run the 10,000 metres. Many runners would have been unable to focus. Not her.

In the midst of all her tribulations, Liz won the race, improving her personal best at the distance by fully twenty seconds. This despite stomach cramps.

Liz's old best had been the Scottish record. Now, two days after her twenty-second birthday, she was the UK all-comers record holder at the very distance Harry had predicted would one day be her best.

This was just prep, of course, for the big race two months later in Edinburgh, the first ever women's 10,000 metres of the Commonwealth Games. On the night before the race Liz rang her father from the athletes' village and told him she was looking forward to it. She was confident. 'There is only one girl I have to worry about,' she told him, 'and that's the New Zealand girl.' But, yes, she confided, she did have butterflies in her stomach. She was trying to ignore them.

His girl, Martin knows, is always nervy. Better not to upset her any more. Her granddad was buried yesterday. Martin had half intended to tell her, but decides to keep the news from her until the race is over. Best not to shock Elizabeth.

'She had been away for the week staying in Edinburgh with the Scottish team. Her granddad had died and been buried and she didnae know till after that race.' Her granddad, who had had a long and happy life, would understand. He was always eager for his runner to win.

Hanging up the phone, Martin keeps thinking about his daughter in Edinburgh all week, alone. He wishes they were going to the race to see her but there's no money to spare in this family. They never go to Elizabeth's races. This time he would like to be there.

In the morning, Martin says, 'Betty' – or maybe it was Betty's idea – 'why don't we go down to Edinburgh and watch our Elizabeth in that race?'

These Commonwealth Games have been a disaster for Scotland. Even before the Games opened, whatever could possibly go wrong has. Too little money threatened calamity until the financier Robert Maxwell stepped into the breach. Then there was a surplus of politics, a boycott by the Africans to show their irritation at Mrs Thatcher's lax attitude towards South African sanctions and Britain's continued backing of Zola Budd.

So miserable and messy was the whole situation that even after the Commonwealth Federation declared Zola ineligible for the Games a fortnight before they opened, and Zola withdrew (on the grounds that she had a sore hamstring), there were still doubts that the Scots would achieve the victory of staging the Games's opening ceremony.

So far the Games themselves have been a rout for the hosts. Few medals, none gold, the best contenders having come and gone with tails between their legs instead of tales of glory. Yesterday in the rain Yvonne Murray had let gold and silver slip out of her fingers in the last minutes of the 3000. Yvonne lives so close to Edinburgh that Meadowbank is virtually her home stadium. You could have cut the gloom with a knife.

Again, today, the sky is granite grey.

John Anderson, the Scot who is coaching the English girls' team, is sitting out of the drizzle about halfway up in the covered stands. Beside Anderson is Dorothy, the woman who is to be his wife. Anderson has coached all three Davids – Bedford and Moorcroft to world records, Jenkins to the European title. Today he and Dorothy have good seats, with a clear view of the finish, directly above the hundred-metre line of the track.

Margaret Whitbread, the javelin coach whose daughter Fatima is competing, sits nearby. Further on is Peter McColgan, still in his green and white Northern Ireland track suit. He finished out of the medals in the steeplechase, but has higher hopes for Liz.

In the open stands where the tickets are cheap Martin and Betty Lynch, bundled into warm jackets, squeeze into a place on the hard benches. Here the crowd is braving the drizzle.

The 10,000-metre race is about to start. Hunching forward, Liz waits for the pistol to fire.

Looking down at her, Anderson sees a long-boned young athlete looking good. At five foot seven inches, Liz weighs seven and a half stone, very little of it fat. The starter fires, and Liz becomes a bullet exploding into the lead.

'That's our daughter,' Martin says to the people next to him, who look dubious.

'Yes, she's ours,' Betty confirms. 'The Scots girl, the one in front.'

'Come on, Elizabeth!' Martin Lynch shouts as the New Zealander Anne Audain surges past his daughter into the lead.

'Come on, Liz!' Betty shouts, clutching Martin's fingers tightly, afraid because the New Zealand girl keeps going faster.

Thirty-one-year-old Audain is the favourite, as they both know from Liz, and Martin knows from the athletics magazines he now reads carefully. In Brisbane, at the previous Commonwealth Games, Audain ran the 3000 metres and was crowned Commonwealth champion. Now she is making good money on the American road-race circuit where they don't pay you for losing, do they?

Betty gnaws her lip.

Martin and Betty's Uncle Alec, who has come down too, look worried. The people near them in the crowd – at least the ones who believe she is their daughter – look positively uncomfortable, but Liz herself looks fine. The only problem is that she is still running second, right behind Anne Audain, but second, lap after lap after lap. Why doesn't Liz pass her?

Wait, Liz tells herself. Hold back for the perfect moment. Because in a race if you go to the boil too soon you can run out of steam. Oh, I want to go, I want to go, Liz tells herself, tempted to make a run for it every time she rounds the track. But she doesn't want to die at the end like Yvonne Murray did because she went for it too soon. The secret of racecraft is choosing the moment. But with the Scottish crowd cheering her forward it is hard to hold back.

As Liz deliberates, Audain puts on the speed. Suddenly there is a terrifying chasm of five metres between her and Audain. Liz digs deep and traverses the chasm. The crowd cheers, lifting her, urging her forward. But Liz again plants herself just behind Audain's shoulder.

Many in the crowd are disappointed. Not John Anderson. As Liz holds back, showing a mental toughness to match her physical strength, he begins to get excited. 'That's one athlete I'd like to coach.' He leans closer to Dorothy. 'She's talented, Dorothy. With the right coaching, that girl could go all the way.'

Ten laps to go, nine. Before the race people like Christine Haskett told Liz, 'you should get a medal at least.' She didn't say she was expecting silver *at worst*. Seven laps, six. Wait. She doesn't want to blow it at the last minute like Yvonne did.

Five laps. The rain has slackened to a light drizzle, but her shorts are already soaking. Four laps. Hold for the perfect moment. It comes two laps from the end. But Audain has been awaiting the perfect moment, too. Now she begins to pull away, opening up a gap of four, five, six metres.

'Come on, Liz!' shouts Martin Lynch, and as if in answer Liz begins to close the gap.

'Come on, Liz!' shouts John Anderson, as again Audain rallies. The English television commentator is predicting Audain's victory as Liz catches up to a point just behind Audain's seemingly impassable shoulder.

'Now!' shouts Anderson.

Now, Liz tells herself. *Now*, and she surges past Audain into the lead. A flash of lightning lights the sky. The noise of the crowd becomes a roar as Liz runs four, five, six metres clear.

'The Scots girl can't keep this up,' says the English television commentator. 'Audain will pass her soon.'

'Liz,' the crowd is chanting. 'Liz, Liz, Liz.'

'Liz!' Betty and Martin and the strangers around them shout. 'Come on, Liz!'

The energy of the crowd moves her legs forward, pushing her forward as Audain fights back, a brave fight, Liz as bravely holding on, still in the lead.

Less than 600 metres left. She looks back. Audain is no closer. You have her, Liz tells herself, you have her. She's not accelerating. You have her. The bell rings, one lap to go. Liz unleashes everything she has left. At last, she is going hell for leather. The crowd is on its feet.

'Come on, Liz!' Martin Lynch and everyone around him shout.

'Come on, Liz!' Anderson shouts, with the rest of them standing.

'Come on!' yells Dorothy.

This feeling as she leads the race, the crowd roaring her home, this amazing and wonderful feeling, I've never felt anything like this before, Liz realizes. Never. The crowd embraces her with their cheers. Prince Andrew is there among them.

Even if I win Olympic medals it can never be more satisfying, she is thinking as the crowd roars and she crosses the line victorious.

As Liz began the lap of honour her team-mates flung their arms about her and strangers showered her with patriotic gifts. Exuberant, elated, Liz Lynch accepted them all and ran, Lion Rampant in one hand, Saltire in the other, draped in the blue and white of the flag of Scotland, the cross of St Andrew. The crowd followed her with its eyes and its heart, its voice rising in a joyous crescendo. Scotland's one gold medal at Scotland's Commonwealth Games, Scotland's one true heroine, Liz Lynch, bonnie and bold.

What she was feeling as she ran this extraordinary lap of honour, so unlike those she had run for her teacher Mr Kearns, was almost too complicated to form into words. Full of happiness, smiling as she ran, this girl who seldom smiled, running round till she found an equally elated Peter, clasped his hand and then ran on.

Now almost every Scot in the stadium was standing, and many were in tears. It was a great day for Scotland. Liz Lynch had showed the world and in particular the old enemy from the south what Scots were made of.

She runs on, still marvellously elated, towards the uncovered stands and there is her dad. She sees him for the first time, jumping over the barrier on to the track. She runs into his arms, and he lifts her into the air.

Everything has changed now.

On the victory podium Liz is the centre of attention, celebrated by the whole of the Commonwealth, those in the Meadowbank Stadium and those listening on the World Service and watching on TV as the official pronouncement resounds: 'The winner of the gold medal and the 1986 Commonwealth Games Champion, women's ten thousand metres, Liz Lynch, representing Scotland.'

Again the crowd goes wild. Liz's arms rise into the air, a spontaneous gesture of triumph and delight. Her finishing time in the race of 31 minutes 44.42 seconds set a new Scottish, a new British and a new Commonwealth record for the distance. Above the trumpeting applause bagpipes play.

In Whitfield, especially in Inveresk Crescent, especially in their block of flats, there is tremendous excitement that Betty's girl has won the gold, even set a new record.

'That will show them that there's more than criminal records come out Whitfield,' announces one of the neighbours. 'A tomboy Liz was before she went to America, and now there she is on telly, Martin and Betty's youngest, the toughie, crying, her tears welling up and spilling over when they put that gold medal round her neck.'

Liz isn't even embarrassed. 'Anne Audain, the silver medallist, and Angela Tooby, who got bronze, bet me seventy-five pounds that I'd cry at the medal ceremony,' Liz says. 'I didn't think I would, but the crowd were something else and "Scotland the Brave" sounded so wonderful, and I felt so good.'

There will never be another day like this one, Betty Lynch is thinking. Never. Winning here in Scotland with her own people and her own folk down about her.

'The stadium full of people shouting my name,' Liz says, 'clapping, it was just so overwhelming, just totally unbelievable. I don't think I'll get that atmosphere ever again in my running career.'

'You only had to be alive and in Meadowbank Stadium, or near a TV set or a daily front page to get caught up in the delirium,' reported the usually restrained *Times*.

'I'm still on a high,' Liz confides to Des Lynam at her first television studio interview, her dangling earrings larger than the tentative, little-girl's voice that would soon disappear.

'You looked supremely confident.'

'It's so natural for me to go the longer distance that I regard the ten thousand as a bonus. I don't even train for the distance, I train for the fifteen hundred and the three thousand.'

'Will you have time for a wee dram to celebrate?'

'Aye,' she says, not mentioning that it will be a wee dram of water. She will be staying in Edinburgh with the team for a few days till the Games close. 'But tomorrow I've got to start training because now it's the European Championships coming up.'

'We all wish you good luck,' Desmond Lynam says. He is wearing a tartan tie.

In Dundee that night Martin and Betty Lynch pop into the Logie Club for a drink. 'It was incredible,' says Martin. 'Everything stopped when we went in. You'd have thought we won the gold medal. Even the band stopped playing.'

Everything is going to be different now, Martin and Betty realize.

'She's done it all against the setbacks,' says her proud father. 'She's shown real character. Liz is something *very special*.'

There is more than one toast that night to Liz, and everyone is pleased that at last she is getting the recognition she deserves. She's a good lassie, isn't she?

'And I'm convinced,' says her mother, 'nothing will ever change her.'

8

In with the Big Girls

There had been one awkward moment in Edinburgh. At the press conference hastily arranged for her by Scottish officials, Liz told the media that she owed her victory to her team-mates at the University of Alabama, 'for giving me the support that I didn't get in Scotland.

'When my coach died I was left in the lurch. I tried to get sponsors, but it's like there were only two or three athletes that anyone cared about in Scotland.'

The Scottish team managers shifted uneasily in their seats.

'I might actually get some invitations to races now.' Her words were pointed. The Englishmen from the nationals were writing them all down.

The man from the *Glasgow Herald* kept listening. 'Few people really believed in me, really believed that I could win, except for my immediate family and a few friends. They had faith and I did it for them.'

As the press conference ended and the journalists filed out, it occurred to one of the hacks from south of the border that for her own good someone should tell this girl the facts of life, one of them being that press conferences are by no means moments of truth.

For her part, Liz was taking the media attention in her stride. So far they weren't writing anything nasty about her or anything seriously untrue. More disconcerting at the moment was the other penalty of fame: the loss of anonymity.

In Dundee, when she turned up at the Polysport complex where ever since her return from America they had been letting her work out in the weights room for free, she was besieged by well-wishers. It happened again when she turned up for business as usual at the centre where she was signing on for unemployment benefit, and if she had stopped to shake each hand that had been proffered on her first training run she would have been out there till midnight. 'Everyone wanted to say well done. Before I won, all I'd get was abuse. Now it's, "Hi, Liz, how're you doing?" They're really interested and I get a lot of support.'

Yes, everything would be different now. Very different. The prospect was enthralling. And if it was sometimes trying to have to thank so many strangers for their congratulations, or to sign autographs, the disadvantages of fame by no means outweighed the advantages.

She had returned home to a heroine's welcome. Dundee's two bronze medallists owed their victory parade through city streets lined with cheering Dundonians to Liz. Standing on the upper deck of an open-topped bus with her entourage of friends and family, Liz didn't mind the gusting forty-mile-per hour winds ruffling her hair one bit.

Bagpipes played. Drivers honked. Regulars came out of the pubs and saluted Liz atop her passing red bus. Officials awaited the heroine at the entrance to City Chambers, where a band piped 'Bonnie Dundee'.

When the celebrations were over and Liz arrived at Whitfield, the whole block of flats was decked with bunting and a giant banner of congratulations greeted her.

There were a dozen years between their ages and there had been bad blood between them, but because they were both Scots the officials in their wisdom had decided Liz and Christine Haskett Price would room together at the meeting. It is often thus and was more so in the old days.

It was not as dire as it might have been since Harry's first star, Liz's erstwhile bitter rival, was now used to being at the back of the field in Liz's races. Christine, a former European junior silver medallist and senior UK 3000-metre champion, had been tenth at Meadowbank, but she had the distinction of being the only athlete, male or female, to have also competed sixteen years earlier in the 1970 Commonwealth Games, an unheard-of longevity.

Liz had been hastily asked to compete at this international meeting – Christine thinks it was at Hendon. Neither Liz nor Christine would remember this minor race at all except for two things. One, it was the only time they would ever share a hotel room. Secondly, because of a chance meeting with someone else.

Over breakfast, John Anderson passed their table and stopped to say hello. Anderson was *the* top Scottish coach. Christine introduced him to Liz. Pleasantries were exchanged and Anderson, who knows a lot of people, walked on to talk to someone else.

'That's the coach Harry had in mind for me,' Christine told Liz. 'When I left Dundee, Harry wanted me to get in touch with John Anderson, but he was Scottish National coach at the time and I guess I felt a bit intimidated.'

Liz's blue-grey eyes now followed Anderson across the room with interest. Anderson didn't look back. The serious wooing would begin in Stuttgart.

Meanwhile, Liz defeated Zola Budd in a 2000-metre race at Gateshead. 'I didn't get any great pleasure out of beating Zola. Certainly no more than if I were beating Yvonne Murray, but it is nice to show that she isn't invincible. The media tend to put her on a pedestal.'

For Liz, 'beating her was just another step in the right direction – beating Ingrid Kristiansen would be another'.

The gaunt Norwegian was the woman who dominated distance running. She was favourite to win the European 10,000-metre Championship in Stuttgart. Liz was eager to meet her, but not yet. 'I was tired mentally and physically.' Only four weeks after Meadowbank, it was too soon for another top-level 10,000.

Far better, Liz reasoned, to run the shorter 3000-metre race in Stuttgart. But British officials were insisting she run both. They had a new star, and she was getting invitations to races all right. Too many.

'A lot of pressure was exerted on me to do something I didn't want to do.' Still hoping she would be spared the 10,000, which she knew she wasn't up to, Liz went to Germany.

Everyone but Tessa Sanderson was there for the Europeans. Like Liz, Tessa had just won Commonwealth gold. Tessa was also the Olympic champion. She had stayed at home, so the story went, because she was injured.

But, said *The Times* somewhat unkindly, 'there is more than a suspicion that her advisors had prevailed upon Tessa not to risk her public image after Edinburgh by coming here and competing against sterner opposition'.

Liz was not a regular reader of *The Times*. Even if she had been, it is doubtful anyone could have persuaded her to behave so tactically. The thought of re-entering the world of top-level British and European athletics was too alluring. Besides, she might win.

Tessa's great rival, the other javelin thrower Fatima Whitbread, who had wept when Tessa's victory left her with mere silver at Meadowbank, was here. So was the other Scot Yvonne Murray as well as the popular British heptathlete Judy Simpson. These championships were without a doubt the most prestigious competition of the year.

As it turned out, Stuttgart's Neckar Stadium would belong to Fatima Whitbread. At roughly the same time that Fatima's picture graced the front page of *The Times* because she had set a new world javelin record, John Anderson, an ex-Glaswegian, bumped into the man from the *Glasgow Herald*.

Doug Gillon was one of the few journalists who had been following Liz Lynch's career closely even before her triumph at the Commonwealth Games. He is an interesting character. Still at the *Herald*, with the only serious beard on the athletics circuit and a Fu Manchu moustache, he is an excellent judge of athletics horse flesh. When Liz can find the time to sit down and write her autobiography – it is gruelling work, as Fatima can tell her – it is Gillon she wants as co-author.

But to get back to Stuttgart. There, not surprisingly, Liz had finished woefully out of the medals in both her races. Gillon remembers asking Anderson shortly afterwards, 'How would you like to coach that athlete, John?'

'She has real promise,' was Anderson's answer, 'and she certainly needs coaching.'

Gillon believes that was the moment at which Anderson first thought *seriously* of coaching Liz. At the time Gillon thought it would be a good match, and still does. 'There is no doubt that John Anderson added speedwork to her training.' Gillon regards Anderson as a good coach and counts him a friend, this despite what has been a very acrimonious divorce between athlete and coach.

But for some time it would be a fine romance, and it was Liz who would get it under way.

Having arrived at the European Championships a winner, now, suddenly, she was a loser, twelfth in the 3000, seventh in the 10,000 metres where Ingrid Kristiansen had been the easy victor. It didn't feel good to be a loser. By some accounts, Liz felt desolate. But almost immediately one of the aspects of her nature that would make her a great champion came to the fore. Remember, when the going gets tough the tough get going.

Liz looked at her finishing time, and she looked at Kristiansen's and at some of the others', and she felt a growing sense of possibility. True, Liz had been very thoroughly beaten. Kristiansen's winning time of 30 minutes 23.25 seconds was a long and unhappy minute and a half ahead of Liz.

But Liz knew she had not been herself in the race. She had felt sluggish, her legs terribly heavy. She had never got properly into gear because indeed it had been too soon to race the distance again. Liz had been right, the officials wrong. Despite the fact that Liz had felt almost lame, with other runners on the track in front of her to chase, her time in the 10,000 had been much better than she suspected – 31 minutes 49 seconds, not far off her time at Meadowbank.

So she wasn't discouraged. 'I learned a hell of a lot from the European Championships, most important of all being that people who I once considered unbeatable are in fact quite within striking distance.'

Anderson interpreted the results quite differently. Even at her then best, he knew, Liz could not have made an impression at the Europeans. 'She'd been totally outclassed in both the three thousand and the ten thousand metres.' He was sad for her but by no means surprised. 'It's a lovely fairy tale to win the gold medal in front of the home crowd, as she had at Meadowbank, but she had had no competition there. In Stuttgart, we're talking about in with the big girls, and there was a reckoning.'

If Liz had been something of a princess at Meadowbank, now she was a bit of a Cinderella. Still, unlike Anderson, Liz believed in fairy tale endings and, being Liz, she didn't mope, she did something about it right there in the Stuttgart athletes' village. What she needed was a coach. She found one.

'This slip of a girl appeared from nowhere on the other side of Judy Simpson,' recalls Anderson, 'and just joined us on the walk to the dining room which was half a mile, I suppose. I knew who she was but she was talking to Judy, and Judy is a big girl so I hardly actually spoke much. When we got to the dining room, she peeled off.

'Judy and I had our meal, breakfast I think it was, came back out again probably three-quarters of an hour later, and this girl joined us again. She had to be waiting.

'When we got back to the quarters, we stopped and chatted for a few minutes, it was polite chitchat, and then Judy said she had to go off and write some letters, or she had to do something. So I expected Liz to peel off as well then. I was going to go back to my place, but Liz said, "Can I have a talk to you?"

'"Yes, course."

'"Could we talk about training?"

'"Yeah, do you want to come back to the flat and have a chat?"

'"Aye, all right."

'So we went back and had a conversation for a couple of hours, maybe more. When we chatted about her training initially, it was quite apparent that she had been neglecting her short speedwork and that is fatal. You can't hide from the faster athletes these days, not even at ten thousand metres.'

Anderson told Liz she was doing too many long runs. What she needed were shorter ones of better quality.

'She could run for ever, and she had an appetite for training and running but there was no structure to it, there was no balance to it, there was certainly no sense of dealing with the anaerobic side as well as the aerobic side. She didn't know anything about the technical side of running.'

During this time, 'she effectively asked me – she asked me – to coach her'.

Anderson's answer was to write out a training schedule then and there. 'Let's give it a shot,' he says he said.

In Liz's memory of that moment, ten months later, there is even poetry: 'That day in Stuttgart when he said I was the athlete he most wanted to coach has changed my whole career.'

By either version, as coach and athlete they were seemingly betrothed.

Nonetheless, when a local sponsor came up with money for the flight Liz flew back to Alabama early in September for the autumn university term. Her scholarship, which it appears had not been withdrawn, had three years to run. But the team wouldn't train with her lest she taint them with her professionalism. She says she was allowed to train apart from them on the far side of the track. It was horrible. She was being treated like a pariah, untouchable.

A week later she was back in Dundee. It was final now: after three years in America she was staying home. She had been to the wars and was sullied. Only her Scots accent was untainted. She still had that intact.

'Aye.' She grinned. 'You only Americanize if you allow it to go to your head.'

Now they wanted to know why she had gone to America, and Liz saw no reason to mince her words. 'There was nothing for me here,' she said. 'There was no support from my local council, or the athletics bodies or anyone. They're only interested in the Coes and Budds, not the up-and-coming.

'It makes me wary,' she went on. 'I'm the kind of person who doesn't forget. If people refused me two years ago, I don't forget that, and when they approach me now I tell them they should have helped me when I needed it.'

She put herself totally in Anderson's hands.

Their major objective would be the World Championship in Rome the following year. 'I was very eager to run the ten thousand in Rome and I couldn't have had a better year of preparation. Through the season, I concentrated on speedwork under the ever-watchful eye of my coach, John

Anderson, and my efforts were rewarded with personal best times.'

The seeds of their divorce, however, were already present in their first long conversation. There would be a clash of egos, a growing difference of opinion about where credit was due. When Liz told Anderson about her past training, she gave full marks to Harry. In fact, one of the things she liked most about Anderson was that he reminded her of Harry.

'When I met John, he was so like Harry Bennett that we got on so well. It was just like Harry again talking to me.'

In reality Anderson was very unlike Harry. He was fiery, strong-willed, even wilful – more Liz in personality than Harry.

Anderson saw Harry as a lesser coach than himself: 'Harry Bennett who had been her mentor in Dundee had actually been a protégé of mine. So I knew Harry very well. He had come along to my coaching sessions and I knew Harry and Harry's background, and he was a nice man.'

Anderson was right about both points. Harry was a nice man, and Anderson was a more distinguished coach. Harry would have been the first to say so. But Liz would never forget what a crucial role Harry had played in her life, and sometimes Anderson would. She would always feel Harry had made her what she was. As a coach, Anderson would feel he deserved the credit. Sometimes to some people it would almost appear as if he felt he deserved more credit than Liz did. This, of course, was not the case. Unfortunately people frequently mistake appearances for reality.

Since Liz lived in Dundee and Anderson didn't, he coached her mainly by telephone and by post. Odd if you are coaching the javelin, for example, but in a non-technical event like Liz's it is generally accepted that there is no problem with long-distance coaching, provided communication is good. Anderson had coached several of his other athletes at a distance, among them Liz's teacher Phil Kearns.

Liz and Anderson communicated frequently. 'Hardly a day ever went by when she didn't phone me, and sometimes these phone calls were very lengthy indeed. Occasionally she'd phone me two or even three times in one day.' His phone bill went up drastically, too.

Liz's version was slightly different: 'He sends me up a training schedule in the post, and every second or third day I write or telephone him to let him know how it's going.'

She wasn't completely happy: 'It's not ideal but there is no one in Scotland I think is good enough and who I'd feel confident enough to train with. Yes, it's lonely and yes, I do get fed up but once I am out I get great satisfaction from running – I'm addicted to it. And any time I'm feeling really down, my family manages to get me out of the dumps.'

To see her coach, Liz travelled to London where he worked or to Coventry where his fiancée Dorothy had her physiotherapy practice and a house big enough for long-term visitors. Soon Liz would be going south monthly. Training with the world record holder David Moorcroft, Judy Simpson and the rest of Anderson's squad was a lot different from being on her own in Dundee. Sometimes she stayed with Anderson and Dorothy for a week at a time. Later she would also bring Peter McColgan.

'Liz will be the greatest distance runner of all time,' Anderson told anyone who would listen.

By February 1987 Liz had more sponsorship, albeit modest. Once a month British Midland Airways would fly her free on the round trip from Edinburgh to see her coach.

Nor was the weather allowed to hamper Dundee's favourite daughter. With ice and snow gripping the roads and the track, the call went out over local radio for someone, somehow, to help Liz train. The manager of Dundee United offered the cinder track around the club's football pitch, which had undersoil heating.

Although it would never seem to Liz that she had ever received enough support – years later she would complain about lack of sponsors – the fact was that people in Dundee had always stepped forward to help her when she needed it, as even now they were continuing to do. There were not many grand gestures, though. Liz, already living on the fringes of a grander world, understandably expected more.

The rift with her old club, though, was smoothed over. She

had left the Hawkhill Harriers, feeling let down by the others following Harry's death. Now she rejoined the Harriers, much to the relief of old members, among them Barbara Oliver, who had so regularly driven Liz and Gail Pope to Caird Park for training all those years ago. But now, with Anderson, Liz was in the fast lane, even talking the lingo: 'If I wanted to market "myself" as a product, which seems to be the way sponsorship is going these days, I would have to look towards a move to London.'

In the end she decided to stay close to her family in Dundee. 'For me it's very much a case of there's no place like home.'

At Caird Park a group of the Hawkhill Harriers' best male runners offered to train with her as, when and how she wanted, following her training schedules rather than their own. It made training on track more competitive and less lonely.

Before long there would be a Nike contract which Anderson negotiated, thus getting Liz away from the agent Kim McDonald to whom Liz would return when she left Anderson. McDonald, who is a big-time operator with offices in London and in Manhattan, manages other top athletes like Britain's Peter Elliott and the dark-headed American golden girl who runs in Raybans, Patti Sue Plumer.

Before the end of the year, Liz somehow found the time to go over to Strabane to visit Peter McColgan who was back from Alabama. While she was there he was entered in a serious race nearby in Mallusk. 'I didn't want to be stuck in Strabane on my own all weekend, so I just went along and ran.' She won the women's race decisively against a strong field. 'It really is just a break in the winter routine for me,' Liz said. She was getting used to winning again.

In the few months she had been with Anderson, there was already evidence that she was going from strength to strength. Anderson had cut her mileage but increased the quality of her runs, focusing on building speed. Liz had been wary at first: 'When I first saw the sessions for this winter I thought, Hell, that's a summer session, I'll struggle trying to run distance work off that. But the reverse has happened, I'm much stronger.'

For example, 'This time last year I was doing twelve three-minute bursts, or four two-mile efforts. Now I don't run more than six hundred metres in speed sessions,' she said. 'I am doing much lower repetitions now, but higher quality.' During the winter her track sessions were 4 × 600 metres. 'Whereas before I might have done 4 × 1 mile, now I'm doing shorter reps, running them faster with a longer recovery.'

Her new coach was getting an awful lot of credit for her success. Some of the base must have been there, if not from Harry, certainly from Coach Mitchell.

Less than six months after Anderson had begun coaching her, Liz was featured in *Athletics Weekly* which had written about her before but never at such length. 'With John Anderson, renowned motivator and coach to the famous, now calling the shots,' wrote Nigel Whitefield, 'Liz is developing a new philosophy which aims to concentrate on cultivating a respectable speed base.'

'My knees might be disintegrating,' Liz quipped at the mention of 'philosophy', 'but my mind is still active!'

As Anderson willingly explained: 'If you are going to be the best in the world at 10,000 metres, you have to be damn near the best at 5000, and not far off top British standard for 800 and 1500 metres.' With this in mind, Liz would be running shorter distances faster, in her training.

Anderson was generous in his praise of her: 'I think it's worth pointing out that she is as talented as any athlete I have encountered in more than twenty years of coaching at international level – and I am not given to exaggeration.'

Although, soon after, it was Liz's picture on the cover of *Running* magazine, the article almost seemed to be about John Anderson. 'I had to explain to her that my approach to training may be somewhat radical compared to what she'd been used to.' He had had to talk the twenty-two-year-old into winter speed sessions. 'I persuaded her to give it a shot on a trial basis.'

Then, like the veritable convert, she wanted to keep the sessions orthodoxly even when they were no longer suitable. Said Anderson, 'When you run well, you get enthusiastic about it – I can't get her to change the programme now.'

Later, when Anderson spoke to me and represented the situation identically, I thought it was because he and Liz were by then at loggerheads. But no, this was how he had always presented their partnership in public. Very likely it was the truth, or in the vicinity of the truth.

Even so, it must have been embarrassing to Liz to see herself in print as, in effect, poor old eccentric Liz, a great pair of legs, but fairly dim.

People quoted more of Anderson than Liz, partly because, as one journalist who had interviewed her in the early days told me, 'She was nice, but shy, and like so many athletes, she was more interested in running than talking.'

Anderson was able, and eager, to explain what he was doing with Liz and why. This was a key to the schedules he gave her. 'The whole programme was elevated – the steady runs became steady runs *plus*, the fast runs became *very* fast. When she found the speed element, we began to tap into a resource that had never been fully utilized. Suddenly she was used to running fast all the time, and running more confidently because she had more of the elements of the good runner available to her – the ability to change pace, to run at a higher sustained speed, and to kick effectively.'

But Liz didn't always do what Anderson told her. He may not have known it, but her former teacher Phil Kearns, whom Anderson had once coached, did.

'He wanted her to do fast work, really fast while doing slow work,' says Kearns. 'And that's how you get injuries. Liz wouldn't do it.' It was only one runner's opinion.

Or, rather, two.

To this day Liz is a very strong one-pace runner, or largely a one-pace runner, though she hates anyone to say so. It's not so damning. Kristiansen was very nearly the same. Kristiansen overcame this limitation of her body – maybe it was a shortage of fast-twitch muscle fibre, or some other anatomical anomaly, maybe a failure of early training – in the same way Liz would, by making herself stronger than all the rest.

Half a dozen years after Anderson gave Liz her first training schedule, the argument would be made by a Russian coach that kick-building worked best with *shorter* recovery periods over the shorter runs, not longer ones. But clock sessions vary.

Without a doubt, with Anderson as her coach Liz's times began to improve tremendously. They were embarking on an adventure that would take them across continents and to great athletic heights. Technically, Anderson was as able a coach as we had in Britain. A talkative man, and often eloquent, Anderson was quoted in articles about Liz to such an extent that it must sometimes have annoyed her. It was not entirely his fault, however, that he was dominating her interviews.

— 9 —

Bali High

On the fabled island of Bali, just off the eastern tip of Java, the sun shines all day every day. In February 1987 Liz and Anderson left behind the snow and gusting gales of Dundee for this tempting tropical island where the temperature tipped into the high eighties. Only six months after she and Anderson had joined forces, they both felt she was ready to meet the biggest of the big girls, Ingrid Kristiansen, for a duel in the sun.

The prize was $30,000, roughly £20,000.

No one British seemed to think it unseemly that the great Ingrid Kristiansen was racing for money, but Liz, it was felt in some quarters, had more interest in filthy lucre than was proper for a young runner at the dawn of her career. The race on the roads of Bali, they felt, would be for gold not glory.

Liz didn't see it that way at all.

Bali is known as 'the morning of the world'. If Liz could win this race against Kristiansen, world record holder, European champion and so much else, it would start the clock ticking towards the noon of Liz's career.

No one outside their immediate circle gave Liz much chance, the wisdom being that this race would be a well-paid holiday for Ingrid, who had worked hard the previous summer winning major races on the track. The idea of Liz taking on Kristiansen head to head seemed to some not so much ambitious as ludicrous. In Stuttgart Liz had not only been defeated by a minute and a half, she had been *lapped* by Kristiansen.

The race in Bali was to be run over the Stuttgart distance, 10,000 metres, which when run on the road rather than a track is spoken of as ten kilometres or 10K. A victory for Liz seemed as unlikely as a huge tidal wave flooding the central Sahara. Greed, it was felt, was swaying the Scot's judgement. As for Anderson, professional pride goeth before a fall.

On the day before the race Liz broke out in a rash. It didn't bode well.

But it was entirely understandable. The hollow-cheeked Norwegian was the pre-eminent distance runner in the world, male or female. Twice winner of the London Marathon – she would win it a third time that spring and yet again the year after – the thirty-year-old world record holder at 5000 and 10,000 metres, in the half marathon and the marathon, was the undisputed queen of the track.

A high-flying professional woman – whose husband Arve often travelled with her in an auxiliary role despite his own fairly high-powered job in an oil company – Ingrid Kristiansen approached her career with the same seriousness as did the great male athletes.

She had no false modesty, either. Like the Viking heroes of old, she would say in advance of battle, 'I am the best, I will win,' or words to that effect. Then she would go out and win, usually in the time she had predicted. Assertiveness, as a whole generation of successful American women runners also knew, posed no conflict to a woman's other roles as a wife and mother. At home Kristiansen baked eight loaves of bread every week and before a race, to calm her nerves, she knitted jumpers for Arve or their four-year-old son Gaute.

Eight years older than Liz, five foot six and a half inches tall, weighing in at seven stone thirteen, she was a quarter of an inch shorter and slightly over half a stone heavier than the now meaner and leaner twenty-two-year-old who – until she'd turned up in Bali – was the last person on Ingrid Kristiansen's mind.

Liz, like every other distance runner in the world, was obsessed with Kristiansen. In their heart of hearts, every up-and-coming distance runner wanted to emulate Kristiansen, to be Kristiansen, which meant to be in the position of Kristiansen, and to attain that you had to knock Ingrid off her throne.

Oedipal stuff, this – what growing up requires every son to do to every father, so the Freudians say. It is also the law of the athletic jungle. If this sounds harsh, remember it is exactly the way in which a field like science advances. The bright young brains come up with better theories that topple their cerebral elders from their university chairs. In this case it is bodies not brains that are superseded. In both arenas the deposed champions, the Galileos and the Sebastian Coes, retain our esteem, so to depose Ingrid would not quite be to murder her.

Came the race.

The gaunt, fair-haired Norwegian and her heiress apparent ran thigh to thigh for the first eight kilometres, neither of them wanting to make a break until nearer the end when the moment was right.

In the heat and eighty per cent humidity of Bali, Liz felt remarkably good. Perhaps it was to the time in Tuscaloosa that Liz owed her energy; perhaps it was to Anderson's new training schedules; perhaps it was both of these combined with the fact that nature had given her the gift of a strong and adaptable constitution, a body which she had tended well. Liz was feeling very good.

So good that without a flick of those blue-grey eyes in Ingrid's direction, at least a thousand metres before anyone expected it, Liz surged forward. Kristiansen, surprised, tried quickly to follow. Liz surged again with the power and persistence of a giant cresting wave, leaving a broken Ingrid Kristiansen beached eighteen seconds behind.

The great champion Ingrid Kristiansen had been roundly defeated.

Ingrid, Liz could see, was very surprised. No one had beaten her outdoors since the autumn of 1985. Turning to Liz she said, 'Well done.'

'And she told me,' Liz recalls, 'I'd got a lot to look forward to at my age.'

This would be the last time the champion would be quite so gracious to the young pretender.

After the race Liz's coach asked, as always, 'How did the race go, Liz? Any problems? Did you feel good?'

'Aye, all right.'

From Bali Liz and Anderson flew to Orlando, Florida. There

would be no lolling about on sandy beaches here, either. No leisurely visit to Disney World. Liz was entered in the Red Lobster 10K Classic. The prize here too was $30,000.

Kristiansen held the world-best time over the course. Busy preparing for the London Marathon, she wasn't in Florida for the race but Liz chopped a twenty-four-second slab off Kristiansen's world-best time of 31 minutes 31 seconds.

Liz and Anderson had planned to fly on to a race in Phoenix, Arizona, but at the last minute Liz withdrew her entry.

'This is a coaching decision,' announced Martin Lynch, now unofficial PR man. 'John Anderson doesn't want her doing too many road races and wants a two-week gap between races rather than a week.'

If, indeed, *he* had cancelled her appearance, it would be because Anderson realized that Liz was more fatigued by Bali and Orlando than he had expected. It was his job to see she didn't get worn down or burned out.

If it was Liz's decision, it could have been for the same reason or simply because she was fed up and wanted to go home. Then – as now – Liz had a penchant for changing her travel plans at the last minute. This impulsive streak, unusual in a person as obsessive as Liz, is an interesting side to a complex character.

She went home. 'I'm not tempted to start flying all over the world but I could if I was greedy enough,' Liz said. 'Over-racing is a short cut to injuries and bad form. Nothing will deflect me from my main aim, which is a gold medal in Rome this summer – not even money.' In which, as everyone knew, she was very interested.

Less hypocritical than most of us on the subject, Liz made no secret of the fact that she was interested in money. At home in Britain, the big stars like Seb Coe, Steve Cram and Fatima Whitbread were being paid £10,000 for each major British meeting. Liz was paid a much lower rate by the British officials. For big money she had no choice but to go abroad. Those two foreign races in February had earned her £40,000 for her trust fund. It seemed a huge amount.

It wouldn't for long.

Liz was obsessed with her running now, but not so obsessed

that she didn't take time to see Peter McColgan. 'I was in the
States. She was competing in Bali. She flew thirty-six hours and
I met her at the airport. I said she'd obviously need a couple of
hours' sleep.

'"No, I'll go for a run," Liz said. She did eight miles. I just
can't understand it myself.'

But he accepted it. He loved her, and he understood her
better than anyone. In those days Liz rarely spoke openly, even
to Peter, about the intensity of her desire to etch her name on
running history. 'She keeps it all inside,' he would say. But he
knew. And admired her for it. He already knew too, I think, that
his running career would never be as important to their lives as
hers.

Flying to Warsaw in March to run in the World Cross-country
Championship just for the hell of it, Liz faced a brilliant field in
bitterly cold weather. Without having bothered to taper off her
training so she would be fresh for this 5000-metre race, Liz in the
blue vest of Scotland finished a very close second.

Ingrid Kristiansen finished *third*.

'I have no right to be disappointed,' Liz said, 'but I am.' Her
old rival Yvonne Murray had finished only sixteenth, but well
ahead of the rest of the Scots. Even that didn't help.

'When I only missed the title by about two seconds,' Liz said,
'I was disappointed. If I had eased down and prepared to run
well, I could have won the title.'

It was, however, not so important a title as the one that was
her and Anderson's main objective this year: the world championship on the track, one of the pinnacles of the sport. The World
Championships would be held at the Stadio Olimpico in Rome
in September, and Liz would run the 10,000. After only a year
in his hands, John Anderson believed Liz capable of winning.
Kristiansen, whom Liz had yet to show any form against on a
track, would still be the one to beat.

It was one thing to win on the roads, which were the bread and
butter of the sport, quite another to win on the track, which
was the caviar. Kristiansen always peaked for the main summer
season. So now would Liz.

She would enter a carefully selected series of races on the road to Rome. These races would put money in her pocket and doubt in Kristiansen's head.

As the season progressed, with an almost military precision Liz set a series of personal bests on the track. One by one, at half a dozen distances, she honed her racing times, lopping two seconds off her 800 metres time, twelve seconds off the 1500 metres. She was running under-distance, short races to sharpen her speed for the big one in Rome.

Meanwhile Ingrid Kristiansen had a sore foot. The bruised heel she had suffered during the London Marathon was so serious and so persistent that it kept her out of action. All spring and summer Kristiansen put in only three sessions on the track. Much of her training had to be done with no weight on the foot in a swimming pool.

Nonetheless, on 13 July Ingrid appeared in Nice for a pre-World-championship tune-up race. You can't win a major championship without tune-ups. They are also a good time to take the measure of the opposition. Liz was there.

The distance they were running on the Côte d'Azur that night was 3000 metres. The Olympic champion Maricica Puica, who had won the famous race in which Zola Budd and Mary Slaney collided, was there too. Liz beat Kristiansen *and* Puica, slicing seven seconds off her own 3000 metres personal best. Her winning time of 8 minutes 38.08 seconds was the second fastest in the world that year.

With Ingrid injured and Liz now at a new peak, the British press named Liz the favourite to win in Rome. 'I would never underestimate Ingrid, though,' said Liz. 'She's a great athlete who always manages to get herself up for the big championships. Nothing is certain except that I could not have had such a successful season so far without the help of John Anderson.'

It was a mutual admiration society. 'Liz is an athlete of colossal talent, tremendous capacity for work, and a marvellous tenacity. She's a delight to work with,' said Anderson. 'Race after race, it's all falling into place as we planned.'

But nothing seemed to be right about Rome. Soldiers clutching loaded Kalashnikov rifles and pistol-toting *carabinieri* had been with them from the moment the team disembarked at Leonardo da Vinci Airport. The soldiers were on alert at all times, expecting terrorist attacks. Rome was also in the grip of a heat wave.

As Liz sat in her room in what was euphemistically called the 'athletes' village' awaiting her race, which was not for a fortnight, she felt a growing unease. And there was little to do all day besides feel nervous. The so-called village was just two mediocre hotels fenced off for the duration.

'This,' remembers Liz, 'was patrolled by security guards at all times.'

From the athletes' point of view, the armed guards surrounding the Princess Hotel had the advantage of keeping the media out, but the security arrangements, as Linford Christie did not hesitate to say, could have been much more sensitive. 'A searchlight which they shone' was 'lighting up not only the surrounding countryside in their search for Red Brigade terrorists, but our hotel rooms as well.' At the back of the hotel there was a snoring generator designed to awaken the deepest of slumberers.

All this engendered a stalag mentality in the British athletes, but there were no thoughts of escape. It was just too stifling and hot. The team grumbled and hid from the sun in the bowels of the Princess.

'The hotel,' says Christie, 'was just awful and the food provided was worse.' The team had arrived eight days before the championships began. 'We were cramped in our hotel rooms and when it rained the water came in.'

One of the athletes' complaints was that the mattresses on the beds were too soft. 'Some were able to get boards to put under,' says Liz, 'but the unlucky ones, myself included, just put the mattresses on the floor.'

Liz tried hard to count her blessings: 'Air-conditioned rooms made life that bit more bearable.' Liz was sharing with fellow ten thousand metres runner Angela Tooby.

Tooby was driving her wild with unsolicited reports of how well the opposition were running on the training track. Liz would try never to room with the Welsh girl again. You expect tension in the days leading up to a major competition. Liz felt it, and something else. 'It was hard on athletes like myself who were racing at the end of the games as it was very boring hanging around the hotel trying to kill time.'

What was needed was a programme of guided tours of one of the great seats of Western civilization. Even the least artistically inclined athlete could appreciate Michelangelo's Sistine Chapel ceiling. There were no sight-seeing tours. Liz felt strongly enough to complain about this as well as everything else in *Today's Runner*. 'Nor was there any kind of entertainment whatsoever.

'The local cafeteria,' she says, 'was the main focal point where athletes could sit and chat for a few hours just to get out of their rooms.'

They tried to eat sparingly, though. 'Everything was cold and dished up with olive oil, and there was very little variety. It was pasta all the time with some meat that was supposed to be beef or turkey.'

Only a year later Liz would insist on precisely this sort of high-carbohydrate (high potato, high pasta), virtually all-vegetarian diet (which she now follows).

But in Rome she certainly wasn't simply being picky: 'The fruit was also badly bruised and totally unripe. One day, for instance, one of the guys picked up a peach only to find a maggot in it. The second fruit contained another, as did the third. That was it for me – no more fruit!'

It wasn't as though the Italians were complete blunderers. They had provided excellent food and accommodation at a different hotel for the middle-aged delegates from the International Amateur Athletics Federation.

The Stadio Olimpico left less to be desired. In the view of the British official Tony Ward, it was 'built on gladiatorial lines. Any self-respecting Christian arriving on a time-warp would immediately feel at home.'

Any self-respecting athlete, however, could not but be pleased with this and the adjoining stadium's facilities. There were three tartan tracks to choose from. Only three miles from the Princess Liz found a park, which she hoped would be perfect for the long runs. It wasn't. Uneven underfoot, it was not suitable for fast tempo runs.

'So I did most of those on the hard shoulder of a nearby motor-way. This turned out to be unhealthy with the exhaust fumes from passing cars.'

The nasty blisters Liz got in the qualifying round, which didn't help her disposition, were the talk of the village. Betty Lynch would be shocked at the sight of them even days after the final. 'I've never seen blisters of such a size as those on Liz's feet. She deserves a medal for having the courage to run with them.' So now she and Ingrid were more evenly matched. They both had bad feet. Every day Liz was more eager to get her 10,000-metre final over with and to get out of Rome. Not the best of mental attitudes, but not her fault.

The night before her race she couldn't sleep, and for the first time in her life took a tablet from the team doctor: 'Something I will never do again because I don't like the idea of taking pills and things and putting tablets into my body.'

Her race the next day wasn't until seven p.m. Liz stayed in her room all day, 'really trying to waste the time'. Angela was there to talk to, always a mixed blessing. There were some books and crosswords. It was hard to concentrate. The bus to the stadium left at four-thirty. It was a forty-five-minute journey. And then it was time to prepare herself.

'As I was warming up I suddenly felt very scared. I was dreading the race for some reason.' She lined up for the start. There was no reason to be scared. She had beaten Ingrid more than once at shorter distances, and at 10,000 metres on the island of Bali.

As the race began, Liz glanced only fleetingly at blonde-haired Kristiansen running beside her at the front of the pack. It was rainy, but hot. Ingrid was racing bare-handed instead of in her characteristic white cotton gloves. At first the pace was fairly slow, which suited Liz whose push was planned for the final stage.

'Then, to my surprise, Ingrid Kristiansen began to move away.' The pack let her go, sure that she would soon have to slow down. 'All week in the newspapers there had been stories of Kristiansen and her injury troubles. I now realize she must have had the best public relations man in the business working for her, but at the time we all thought she would blow up.'

By 2000 metres, Kristiansen had a fourteen-second lead, a gargantuan eighty metres on the track. At 3000, Liz was leading the pack and Kristiansen was sixteen seconds ahead of them. The other athletes were taking the free ride behind Liz, none of them offering to do the work of leading in an effort to catch Kristiansen, whom they still half hoped had gone out too fast and would be stopped by exhaustion, or by her injury.

They were making it easy on Kristiansen, but hard on Liz, 'clipping the back of my heels and generally jostling around, making it a rougher race than it needed to be'.

Shortly after the 8000 metres mark, Kristiansen increased her lead to twenty seconds. Liz, despite her painful blisters, was still poised for silver.

On the very last lap the others surged past Liz. One of the Russians took silver, a German took bronze. It was disastrous. Even though her time of 31 minutes 19.82 seconds was a personal best by nearly twenty-two seconds, and a new British and a new Commonwealth record, Liz felt terrible. 'I was fifth, just a second behind the other Russian, Bondarenko.'

Although Liz didn't know it yet, Olga Bondarenko, she of the short stature and sturdy Slavic cheekbones, would become as haunting a rival as the fair-haired Norwegian who was now world champion.

'All credit to Kristiansen,' Liz said, in concluding the column she wrote in *Today's Runner*, 'but I take issue with people who call her the greatest female athlete in the world because I think I'm capable of beating her. On the day, I ran a bad race.'

Fifth was ignominious when you arrived the favourite. But Liz made no mention of the blisters.

It was no comfort that virtually the whole British team had had a bad race. Fatima Whitbread's was the only gold medal. This time it was Fatima's picture that made the front page of the papers. Fatima was Britain's sole world champion. It would not always be thus.

There were two equally golden titles in athletics, the World Championships and the Olympics. Liz intended to be ready for the queen of the track next year at the Seoul Olympics.

Meanwhile, Liz Lynch had something else on her mind, something important.

Her wedding.

— 10 —

Body and Seoul

Early in the morning Liz was up and out as usual for her ten-mile run. Less usual was the visit to the hairdresser where a photographer from the local newspaper popped in for a shot of Roslyn wielding the hairdryer. Liz also had her make-up done. The third of October 1987 was going to be a very busy Saturday.

A bridal gown and its accoutrements take far longer to get into, Liz was discovering, than do running shorts and a pair of trainers. But absolutely everything had to be exactly right today. It was as important as the Olympics. With every hair and every crinoline finally in place, Liz left for the church. There were sighs of relief when she got there. The wedding was due to start in five minutes.

As Liz walked down the aisle of St Andrew's Cathedral, with pearls at her neck, lace scallops on her long white dress and flowers in her hair, Vi Bennett, Harry's widow, thought she looked perfect, a picture of serenity. She was carrying a trailing bouquet, the pale yellow and pale blue – sort of aqua – roses were shown off by delicate white carnations.

Her two nieces, Sarah and Samantha, were the flower girls. 'The little ones,' Vi Bennett remembers, 'were dressed in white with wee knickers and frills underneath and wee baskets. They were beautiful.'

Karen thought so, too. Liz's big sister was also at her loveliest in the off-the-shoulder aqua bridesmaid's dress she and Liz had chosen together at Pronuptia in Dundee. The shopping for the wedding dresses had been done long before Rome. Peter's sister Jacqueline was the other bridesmaid. All the dresses had been altered to fit perfectly.

Peter awaited his bride in wing collar and tails and that dashing cravat Vi had noticed when he was sauntering down the aisle. Vi thought he looked especially handsome. Harry had worn tails at their wedding. He had looked handsome too.

Peter's brother Aidan, the best man, now proffers the rings. Fleetingly Vi remembers her own brother's part in her and Harry's wedding. A gardener, he had made up the bouquets: red tulips for his sister the bride, pink ones for the bridesmaids.

A double ring ceremony, the two rings joining them equally. That is the kind of marriage those two intend to have.

As Peter slips the ring on to Liz's finger, for just a wee moment Vi, like so many others in the cathedral, remembers the first moment she wore her wedding ring. There were tears shed, smiles, hands clasped, as Peter and Liz become husband and wife. Vi silently wishes them well. May they have as happy a marriage as mine was to Harry, her thoughts shout, happier if they can – and may it last longer.

Outside the church, awaiting the bride and groom on the steps, were young members of Liz's club the Hawkhill Harriers dressed in their club running kit. Forming a guard of honour they crossed their relay batons like swords above the heads of the newly-weds. This was a surprise arranged by Barbara Oliver, who was still setting Scottish records in her age group and still trying to make Liz feel more than welcome at Dundee Hawkhill.

The wedding reception was held in the Queens Hotel, a couple of minutes' walk from the Catholic church. Among the guests was Yvonne Murray, there with the man from *Athletics Weekly*, Nigel Whitefield, who was her fiancé. Sitting at the same table was another well-known Scottish athlete, Linsey Macdonald.

The next day there were pictures in the paper. Liz looked beautiful but the show was stolen by Peter, who appeared every bit the elegant Victorian gentleman.

They spent their wedding night at a hotel. The next morning, Betty Lynch recalls with a smile, 'The man who owned the hotel couldnae believe she was up at seven a.m. on her honeymoon and going out running.'

On the following Saturday they were in America. Liz had a road-racing date in Iowa, and a week later another in Texas. Her honeymoon takings were at least £25,000.

But it was good to get home to their new house, which was not far from Dundee but in a sense a world away. It was in the country, one of three or four bungalows nestled together smack in the middle of a network of winding lanes that seemed almost purpose-built for running.

The village was called Monikie and they liked the name of the Lucky Slap Road. Peter was still a top-ranked steeplechaser, though he was not attracting the sort of attention Liz was. Sometimes they trained together on these quiet roads. The location was one of the reasons she and Peter had chosen the house.

They had moved in two or three weeks before the wedding. Before that they had been living in the second bedroom of the Lynches' second-floor Inveresk Crescent flat. Surveying her new domain, Liz felt good. Now for the first time in her life she had a home of her own. She had well and truly left Whitfield.

There would be no babies, no pregnancy, the *Sun* reported, until well after the Olympics. 'Peter and I have agreed to wait until after the 1988 Games at Seoul before I settle down to become a housewife and mother,' it said she said.

To be sure, Liz liked children and hoped to have many when the time came. The press kept asking her how many, and Liz kept upping the numbers. To one astonished journalist, she said six. But Liz did not see herself as a traditional housewife and mother.

She saw her marriage to Peter as a partnership, and one that would not work unless both partners were involved in running. 'If one half was off competing and enjoying themselves, and the other was at home, then there must be something lacking in their relationship because running really does become part of your life,' she wrote in her column in *Today's Runner*. 'With Peter it's great. He really helps me a lot. He understands the commitment to training and racing, so he pitches in and helps me around the house.'

Peter was good for Liz in a lot of ways. He was the only one who could make her feel loved when she was feeling cantankerous and nervy. 'He understands how I feel before a big race. I always go quiet the day before and keep myself to myself. He knows what I'm going through and understands so he doesn't get upset.'

Even when he did get upset, and he would have been super-human not to sometimes, he put Liz and Liz's race first.

By February, Liz was in America again – back in Orlando, and hoping things would not be different the second time around. The Florida runners were not glad to see her, but *Florida Running* was. 'Sporting a hyphen and a brand-new last name, Lynch-McColgan went into the Red Lobster 10K Classic on 6 February looking for a sign that she had indeed arrived as a world-class athlete.'

She had a lot to prove to everyone and something in particular to prove to herself. 'My coach and my husband have been telling me that I'm in great shape and that I've been training hard. But to me, it didn't feel as if I was training hard. Something was missing, and I was really eager to go out and race and test myself.'

There were 1500 runners in the race. Families, children, club runners and a hard core of elite runners. On paper, Liz was the best in the field, but victory wasn't assured and she wasn't here just for victory. Liz wanted a new world record. The odds of achieving it were, to say the least, slim. Apart from the unseasonable and rather British weather, with a persistent rain, no athlete had ever set a world record on an American road-racing course two years in a row.

As Liz crossed the finishing line at the head of the field in 30 minutes 59 seconds, the excited Floridan announcer, bellowing at the top of his lungs, said, 'Liz Lynch has just set another world record!'

She had sliced eight seconds off the record, becoming the first woman ever to break the psychological barrier of thirty-one minutes on the road. It was a wonderful achievement. Had it replaced the 'something' that was missing?

'Running here today didn't really help me. I know I can go faster. I was really relaxed the whole way. At my best, I think I can run forty to fifty seconds faster. Right now, I think I can be in the low thirties.' She wanted to go faster and she needed to go faster. This need decreased the joy Liz felt in her victory.

Peter had finished twenty-ninth in the men's race.

His wife's prize was $33,000, ten per cent more than last year's cheque. 'Not bad,' said *Florida Running*, 'for an athlete who had only won one road race ever just a year earlier.'

But surely news of the Azalea Run and the Vulcan Run in not-so-far-away Alabama less than two years ago had reached Orlando, even if Liz hadn't told the reporter about the takings on Bali and elsewhere?

What this report in the magazine meant was that *officially* Orlando was her first money race in America. Ever after the count of how much money Liz had earned racing would, because of this sort of omission and others, lag behind the truth.

The Americans had made another mistake. Liz Lynch had not become Liz Lynch-McColgan. Many runners, the world record holder Mary Decker Slaney, for one, adopted a hyphenated or unhyphenated double-barrelled surname. Others had stuck with their maiden name. After striking Olympic gold in Barcelona in 1992 the hurdler Sally Gunnell, whose next big event was to be her wedding, announced she would continue to use her maiden name professionally because it had been so hard to make it famous.

Liz, however, opted to take Peter's name. 'I've decided to make my change of name now, so that whatever I accomplish in 1988 will involve Peter,' she said. 'From now on I want to be known as Liz McColgan, not Liz Lynch.'

The sentiment was sweet, but in terms of both fame and fortune the decision may have been a mistake. The Lynch name was already well known, one of the reasons being that it was short enough to fit easily into headlines. McColgan, as Liz herself would acknowledge later, was a harder name to remember. To this day, many people say 'McCoglan' or 'McCochlan' instead of McColgan. The name Liz Lynch was easier to remember and easier to say.

Ironically, the one runner in Britain who had actually spoken of herself as a 'product' to be marketed threw away one of her most valuable marketing assets, her hard-won product identification. If she had kept the name Lynch, I believe, she would have been a household name long before now.

But the heart has its reasons.

And they must be honoured too.

Less than a month after the wedding, when it was time to plan the new season, Liz was careful to include Peter. 'My coach, John Anderson, my husband Peter and I all sat down together to discuss my training, my approach to racing, my racing schedule.'

In 1988 her main object was the Olympics in Seoul. 'With John's advice and Peter's support, I am sure that the year ahead will be a rewarding one for all of us.' Those last words didn't sound like Liz at all, unless she was trying to unruffle one or the other man's feathers.

Peter was already turning his attention from his own running career as a steeplechaser to his wife's. Anderson still saw Liz only intermittently, except when they were travelling together. Peter helped out on a daily basis. A triumvirate – the runner, the coach and the involved and supportive husband – could work very well. It worked for Kristiansen.

The winter season slid into the summer with a lucrative string of victories. Liz McColgan lost only once on the track, to Yvonne Murray in a 3000-metre grand prix in Nice. There was good appearance money in grands prix.

Far more important to the outcome of the Olympics were the three victories over Kristiansen at 3000, 5000 and, almost unbelievably, at 10,000 metres. On the track, no one had beaten Kristiansen at her preferred distance, certainly not since she had set her first world 10,000-metre record in 1985 at the famous Bislett Stadium in Oslo.

There is a special joy in setting a world record on your home track. The following year at Bislett Kristiansen ran 30 minutes 13.74 seconds, cutting a roast-size slab of 45.72 seconds off her previous time and resetting the world record.

On the Saturday night in Oslo in July 1988, when Liz whizzed ahead of Ingrid and it was clear who would finish first, it seemed that the world of athletics had been turned upside down. Ingrid, a terrible look on her face – is it shock? – even stops short for a moment when she realizes the enormity of what has happened.

'I tracked her the whole way,' Liz said. 'We ran side by side until, with about fifteen hundred to go, I went to the front. She tried to go with me for a lap and a half, but she just couldn't. I believe she stopped but I did not see her.'

Liz and the media had good reason to be euphoric. She had beaten the lioness in her den. There was also $10,000 in prize money, and who knows how much appearance money. It was all to be funnelled into her trust fund.

A few days later her joy was clouded when there were reports that Kristiansen had had a miscarriage. She had not known she was pregnant. At the 9000-metre mark she had felt such a severe stomach pain that she momentarily stopped running, but pushed on to finish second.

Kristiansen had supposedly been injured in Rome. And look what had happened. Now this. Was this PR too? No, it turned out to be true.

The first ever women's Olympic 10,000-metre race was not taking place until 30 September, so Ingrid would have close to three months to recover. For a woman of her fitness, it was felt, that should be sufficient. At the showdown in Seoul we would finally see if she was still the queen of the track.

Unfortunately, Peter had not made the Olympic team. He would not be going to the Games. They had been married less than a year, and now they were facing a separation of almost six weeks. Even before Liz left on the first leg of her journey, the trip down to London, Peter began to miss her. The day she was leaving Liz went out, as usual, for a ten-mile run.

'I said I'd go out with her,' Peter recalls.

'No,' Liz said. 'If you were with me, I'd end up going faster than I want.' Not good for her preparation.

'Just switch off, forget about me,' he said.

But she couldn't.

'Because it's in her nature that she'd have to beat me no matter what. That's just the way she is.'

'I'm so lucky to have a husband who understands what athletics at this level involves,' Liz told the man from *The Times*. 'I'm not always the happiest person strolling about with a smile on my face, especially when I'm tired, and I think Peter has to put up with an awful lot. A husband who wasn't involved in athletics would find it hard to understand why you get so tired and you can't be bothered to do things.'

Liz spent the night before their departure for the Olympics at John Anderson's London flat. Dorothy, the physiotherapist whom he was marrying in November, was there too. John had invited Liz to stay partly to save her the cost of a hotel and the effort of getting herself to the airport, and partly because Anderson felt they could use the time together.

On this latter point, he may well have made a big mistake. The three of them went out to a pizzeria in Rotherhithe. It was a place near John's recreation department office which was next door to the local Labour Party. John had his usual, cannelloni, Dorothy lasagna. What Liz ate on the night is unrecorded.

John was, as ever, talkative.

They ate together, talked together – or rather more often he talked and the women listened, sometimes only pretending to listen. He was a great talker, John Anderson.

Liz, who liked to keep herself to herself the day before a race, was nervous the day before the flight and already feeling the pull of the Olympics. As Anderson's voice with its lilt and its laughter filled her ears, there were some moments when she felt encroached upon and yearned for silence.

The three of them went back to the flat where Liz slept on the settee. A taxi arrived in the morning to take Liz and her coach to Heathrow.

As they boarded the plane, it seemed to John Anderson that all was as it should be between them. Athlete and coach were well melded, close. He was looking forward to the two weeks he and Liz would spend together in the Olympic team's pre-Games holding camp, doing the final sharpening of her speed and confidence.

Anderson was pleased he would be able to spend more time with her than he had been able to at the World Championships. And before she had come down to London, so too was Liz. 'In Rome, he was not on the team and although he was out there it wasn't the same. This time he's on the team.' She sounded enthusiastic. Maybe his being there would make all the difference. Instead of fifth, this time she was hoping for gold.

His athlete, Anderson felt, had had her fingers on the hem of the world championship. What he planned to do at the Nihon holding camp was taper Liz's training so that she could wrap herself in the metaphorically ermine robe of Olympic glory.

On the long flight to Tokyo, Anderson sat with the other officials, Liz with the athletes. Separated as they were by the plane seats, Liz and John didn't really speak on the journey. But as they disembarked from the plane, it seemed to John Anderson that during the flight something had changed between them. He couldn't put his finger on it. Somehow Liz felt far away. It was almost as if the coach–athlete relationship had suddenly entered a new season. Chillier.

There had been pandemonium at Tokyo airport when the famous, not-yet-infamous, Canadian sprinter Ben Johnson stepped off his plane. Three hundred or so media were waiting, though his flight time was supposed to be secret. The paparazzi were not worried whose toes they were stepping on. An old woman was knocked down, her bags sent flying. Policemen with clubs cut a path for Ben's retinue to the exit where a van took off with Ben Johnson's million-dollar legs sticking out of the door.

When Liz arrived, all was quiet on the Eastern front. This was one of the advantages Liz McColgan would later come to realize of not being a big star.

With no bustle, you can take your time about things, talk to whomever. Going through customs, however, Liz and Anderson somehow didn't connect or chat. He couldn't catch her eye as they walked the sixty metres along the corridor that led out of the airport. Nor did he on the sixty-mile drive to the Nihon holding camp, where the British and the American teams and many of the Germans would be staying to train and acclimatize in the weeks prior to their arrival in Korea for the Games.

With its wooden huts, its high fencing and elaborate security – there were rumoured to be terrorists about – Nihon, it immediately struck Randall Northam, looked like a luxurious Japanese prisoner-of-war camp. The editor of *Athletics Today* and the rest of the media were already ensconced when the British team arrived. Everyone was staying in rough-hewn wooden chalets.

But Northam and the other press had been billeted in the chalets on the far side of the complex, which from an athlete's point of view meant that they were out of harm's way.

The mosquitoes were biting despite the huge electrical devices the Japanese had rigged to electrocute them. Confusingly, the noise of the electrical apparatus humming sounded like swarming mosquitoes.

At first glance, most of the athletes thought Nihon was terrific. It looked expensive, and it was. And all the best Germans and Americans were staying there. It felt elite. When the camp wasn't being hired out to international athletes for their pre-Olympic training, Nihon Aerobic Centre was a millionaire's playground. It looked the part. The place had cost a billion dollars to build and nearly everyone was impressed, including Linford Christie.

'The facilities were out of this world,' he says. The 400-metre track was superb. Inside the main three-storey centre, the sports hall and the weights room were state-of-the-art, as were the swimming pool, saunas and Jacuzzis. There was also plenty of room for the team doctors, masseurs and physios. Linford, who is no pushover, called it 'the best training centre I have ever seen'.

Liz was less impressed.

True, the 200-metre indoor track was good, as was the regulation outdoor 400-metre synthetic track. That was terrific for the sprinters. But Liz needed more space, somewhere really to run. The golf course, where it was reputed the greens fee was £250 for a single round, wasn't suitable either. The hills were too steep for training at this point in the season, and there were strange, potentially ankle-spraining bumps and bulges in the ground underfoot.

'Except for the sprinters, the place was no good for training,' says Randall Northam. 'All they needed was a track but a distance runner needed space to run. You couldn't run on the grass. It seemed to be built on volcanic foothills with unpredictable, hidden lumps.'

John Anderson began making frantic phone calls. He needed to find a place with space.

Liz was rooming with Kirsty Wade. Two years older than Liz, dark-haired Kirsty, who held the Commonwealth 800- and

1500-metre titles, was going for gold in both at the Olympics. Kirsty had been born in Scotland to English parents who brought her up in Wales. She had married a Geordie and was living in Newcastle. Liz and Kirsty, who had never shared a room before but certainly would again, got on well. Each had left her supportive husband at home.

Yvonne Murray, who was sharing with someone else, was one of the other athletes staying in that chalet, which was six or seven minutes' walk from the main centre, though you could hop on a courtesy bus if you wanted to. People met up in the dining hall in the centre.

On the first evening, as Anderson was eating his meal, he waved and called hello to Liz. She seemed not to notice. She could not have seen him, he thought.

On the second day much the same thing happened. Liz was keeping away from Anderson. It wasn't as planned, but Anderson didn't worry. The first couple of days were for acclimatizing and they didn't need to see a lot of each other yet.

On the third and fourth day, sure now that she was avoiding him, he began to get increasingly worried. Knowing that Liz's result at the Olympics was more important than his personal pride, Anderson went, uninvited, to visit the chalet Liz was sharing with the others. It was only because of Kirsty Wade that he was even allowed in. When he was admitted, Anderson recalls, Liz was fairly rude to him.

She had often been short with him before.

Now even when they worked on the track she was short-tempered with him. John Anderson felt excluded but he realized Liz was feeling intruded upon. 'She felt I was in her space.' It took a sensitive man to realize that, but he was unable to diagnose the reason.

Liz didn't say what it was that was bothering her, but she was giving him the cold shoulder as Harry Bennett had occasionally done to her. Without saying a word about it, exuding tension, Liz made it plain to Anderson that she was 'in a mood' with him.

He rang home, frustrated. 'I can't get in to see her,' he told Dorothy. 'She changed once she got here, just ignores me.'

To this day, neither he nor Dorothy understands why.

Anderson's memory is of too little access to the chalet and brief visits, of Liz cutting off from him, of being frozen out. 'Ask Kirsty Wade about it,' he said to me.

Kirsty was not eager to bear witness. I pressed her. Was it true that Anderson had been kept out?

'Oh, we saw a lot of John,' Kirsty said. 'I've got a photograph of him asleep in our room. One afternoon he fell asleep on the chair. We saw a lot of John, more than she was used to seeing of him.' Peter McColgan also told me about the photo.

No doubt Anderson had fallen asleep because he was emotionally exhausted. However much he was seeing of Liz, he didn't feel it was enough and it is likely that his memory of one championship has merged with that of another. This appearance of a sudden frost between athlete and coach was to happen more than once.

When finally Anderson and Liz did get together on the Nihon training track, he may have been a bit frantic. But her times were exceptional. That was what really mattered.

Training at the Nihon track was a public occasion. You ran a short distance, your coach timed it, then you did your repetitions – known as 'reps' in the trade – over and over, but you were always in close proximity to the rest of the world's best. Britons, Americans, Germans, they were all using the track at the same time as Liz and Anderson, everyone focused, unphased by the fact that they were training on a foreign track where the lines are in different places.

On a day when Liz was running a timed series of short, sharp 300s, Anderson, looking at his time clock after she had done one of the reps, saw she had been very fast.

'My God, Liz, this is fantastic, this is amazing!' – or words to that effect – he called out to her. 'Liz, you've done an amazing time!'

People like Mary Decker Slaney looked up.

'I think the line's wrong,' Liz said. She was uncomfortable at the fuss he was making.

'There's nothing wrong with the line, Liz. You're just doing very well.'

She ran another rep. The speed work would add a cutting edge to her stamina. Again Anderson timed it. Again it was extremely fast on the clock.

'That's fantastic, Liz!' he shouted. 'That's amazing!'

Everyone turned in their direction. They were all phenomenal athletes, quite a few of them doing world-record stuff.

'I think the line's wrong,' Liz repeated.

'No, Liz, it's not. Your time's amazing!'

'He embarrassed her,' Kirsty recalls. 'She'd just go quiet and walk off. The funny thing was that the line was in the wrong place. They were doing three hundreds and the line was in the wrong place so they were fantastic times.'

But even if the times had been correct, the florid display would have embarrassed Liz. 'I wouldn't have liked it,' Kirsty says. 'Everybody was there. He's a nice bloke, but I do think he's difficult sometimes. He's so enthusiastic.'

Even when they went in the limousine he had persuaded the sponsor to give them to the special site that had become available for long runs, Anderson says, he felt shut out. Liz asked if Kirsty could come along. 'Of course, I said "Yes."' He would do anything that would put Liz in a good frame of mind for her race, even if it seemed unreasonable. As he had once told Daley Thompson, 'Before the race I'll even shine your shoes, but after it you better shape up.'

As Kirsty sat between them in the limousine, chatting amiably first to the one, then to the other, to Anderson she seemed to be the only warm spot in an ice-cold sea. He sometimes felt that without Kirsty there it would not be possible for Liz and him to be in the same car.

'There were times,' Kirsty says carefully, 'when it was a bit tense.'

Liz, by her own admission, is always moody before a big race, and this was a very big race. Distance runners are known for their mood swings and periods of introspection. Anderson, feeling cut off, was struggling to get through to her.

'She didn't cut off from him,' says Kirsty, 'but she needed some space. He sort of put her on edge. She wasn't used to eating and sleeping and thinking with John Anderson. She was used to him being at a distance. There are some people whose personalities do clash. You might get on very well with someone on the phone but you don't necessarily get on on a daily basis.'

Liz was, on occasion, rather blunt. She and Anderson clashed at home too.

'She would answer John back something terrible when she was here,' Dorothy Anderson says, still smarting at the memory. 'She was so off-hand. Gruff. It was always, "Don't you realize this, don't you realize that?" Some of John's other athletes witnessed this. We'd have a house full of athletes. We often do. But John let her get away with it instead of laying down the law.'

From Peter we know of her aggressive words to the coach in Idaho in front of everyone.

'She doesn't suffer fools,' Kirsty says. 'I admire people who do that because they say the things everyone else wants to say, but don't. Liz doesn't think about that, she just says a spade's a spade and that's that.'

Liz has a short fuse.

Even as a child she had a temper. Like the little girl in the rhyme, it would seem, when she's good she's very very good and when she's bad she's horrid.

Well, few heroes are flawless; why should our heroines be?

Nor is Liz herself entirely to blame. One symptom of over-training is irritability. Liz puts in a lot of miles. Sometimes she must be over-tired.

'In everything,' says Dorothy Anderson, 'John backed her to the hilt.' On her account, at Nihon, he had used the sheer force of his personality to talk the sponsors into supplying the limousine.

It was, unfortunately, this very forcefulness that would lead to their clash of personalities. Particularly at a time when pre-Olympic tension made Liz the dourest of Scots, it had seemed invasive. John Anderson is very much there when he is there. In the mood she was in, his presence must have felt as relentless as a toothache.

The gossips in the Nihon camp had good fun with the story of Liz and Anderson. Men are the biggest gossips in the world. Most of the time, though, these hard-core gossipers had even bigger fish to fry. The biggest story of the Seoul Olympics, although no one knew it yet, was going to be muscle-building drugs. Carl Lewis suspected Ben Johnson was on them. Other people suspected Lewis himself.

At night, defying the mosquitoes, some of the press men and a few of the athletes would sit around the swimming pool drinking the low-alcohol beer that was provided, and chatting about the great days and the great men of athletics. This ad-hoc beerfest was an Anglo-American occasion. Punctuated by the slapping of mosquitoes, it sometimes went on late into the night.

There were two favourite subjects: who has the best runners, the Brits or the Americans? And which of them are on anabolic steroids or something else even craftier?

Britain had had the world's best middle-distance runners, the men of the mile, the 1500 and the 3000 metres, Seb Coe and Steve Ovett. The Americans now had many of the world's best sprinters including that one-man army, Carl Lewis.

It is the muscle men, the sprinters, whom everyone suspects of taking steroids, but the strength-enhancing drugs can benefit most athletes. And there are other illicit aids. The American cycling team and a bevy of Italian runners had been caught blood-doping, a method by which you re-inject a pint of your own blood shortly before a race. The extra red cells turbo-charge your internal engine. Some people suspected Ingrid Kristiansen of blood-doping. Other Scandinavian stars had blood-doped. Nowadays the drug EPO does the same job less messily.

'Drug abuse, in the late seventies and early eighties, was probably as rife in Britain as anywhere else,' Tony Ward says in his unusually frank book on Britain's golden athletic decade. For a long time it wasn't even illegal.

'In those days, the taking of drugs was not viewed with the same antipathy as it is now. It was another likely short-cut to success like altitude training.'

But in recent years wiping out drugs had become a holy war. That, at least, was everyone who was anyone's *public* stance. In Barcelona Liz's old college rival from Georgia, the sprinter Gwen Torrence, would angrily voice her suspicion of the fastest female Olympian in the world, the new hundred-metre champion Gail Devers.

Now Carl Lewis, the world's greatest athlete but only the second-fastest man in the world, pointed the finger at secret anabolic potions which he believed were what made the Canadian Ben Johnson number one. Only after the Seoul final would Johnson's drug-taking actually be found out.

In the moonlight of Nihon that night one of the younger, less cynical, of the British journalists says, 'Our lads are above reproach, aren't they?'

In answer an American poses the question: 'When was the last time the British really won at middle distance?'

'That was 1986,' one of the Britons replies. The British men had bombed out of the 1987 World Championships, Fatima winning the only gold medal.

'And when was David Jenkins arrested?'

They all know the answer. The Scot who had become European champion at the age of nineteen in 1971 was arrested for trafficking in anabolic steroids in the summer of 1987. 'Jenks', whom Anderson had coached to his great victory, confessed to taking the steroids himself during part of the time he was competing.

Jenks had left Anderson after failing at the 1972 Munich Olympics, returning to him in 1979 to prepare for a go at Moscow in 1980. It was in the interim, the story goes, that Jenkins took the drugs, which didn't win him anything so he returned to Anderson. When I asked John Anderson if he had known about Jenks' drug-taking, he said that if I were a man he would punch me.

Nearly everyone present around the Nihon swimming pool that night knows that two of the top British male athletes – both of whom would represent Britain at the Barcelona Olympics – went to a cocktail party at Jenkins' house in California the night before he was arrested.

'That proves nothing,' one of the Brits says angrily.

'Absolutely. It *proves* nothing.'

In Seoul, Liz checked into the Olympic Village according to protocol although, *à la* Carl Lewis, she was actually staying at a big hotel. So, of course, was Kristiansen. This was standard procedure for all athletics stars. 'Which was fair enough,' says Kirsty Wade. 'At the village, we were in a room that was noisy, the sheets were thin, the room didn't have any curtains and we were sharing with a lot of people. If I had the opportunity to get out, I possibly would have done.' Kirsty, unfortunately, did not win a medal.

Carl Lewis, who hadn't bothered to check into the village in Los Angeles, made sure he did this time. 'I wasn't going to stay there, but by checking in I would not have to deal with a repeat of the nonsense I heard in 1984. As far as anybody had to know, I was in the village.' He was actually staying with a big entourage at a rented house.

For company at the hotel, Liz only had John Anderson.

Kirsty says, 'I used to run over there in the morning and she used to look after me, you know, make me cups of tea. She's good company. It was great.'

On the morning of the first ever Olympic 10,000 metres final, Ingrid Kristiansen was breakfasting on oatmeal and skimmed milk followed by three pieces of wholemeal toast lathered with strawberry jam, washed down with several cups of coffee. Her usual.

For her part, Liz McColgan had had to send her porridge back to the chef once already this season. He had made it with milk instead of water or, as she sometimes liked it, grapefruit juice. Eventually Liz went into the hotel kitchen and mixed it herself. Nowadays she always travels with a porridge recipe in several languages stowed in her luggage.

Porridge, of course, is made of oatmeal. Eating lots of slow-burning complex carbohydrate – carb-loading – was now the nutritional dogma of the track. Liz had first heard about it in America and it had been drummed into her further by Anderson. She ate no meat and no dairy products, unless she cheated and had an ice cream. For the most part she gorged on baked potatoes. Now she was on much the same diet as Kristiansen, and that evening on the track the world would see whose oats worked best.

Oh, yes: Ingrid was supposed to be injured again. Something else was wrong with her foot, which she said she had injured while training two days before the race. It was always something as the ageing champion fought against the dying of the light. The eight years Kristiansen had on Liz were beginning to hang like an albatross around her neck. Or were they? Liz had been tricked into complacency in Rome. This time she would be very careful.

As they stood on the start line, Liz's face fell into its character-istically dour pre-race pout. She looked miserable, but she was just concentrating.

The world champion looked all right and was as usual wearing white cotton gloves. They were not to keep Ingrid's hands warm, they were to wipe away the sweat of her brow. Liz had no inten-tion of letting her get away this time as she had in Rome. But no matter what happened, Liz planned to run her own steady race, regardless of anyone else's tactics. Ultimately the tortoise, she believed, would prevail over the hare.

As the race began Liz tucked into fourth place, behind the world champion. The pace at first was leisurely, 75-second laps, even one of 77 seconds.

On lap six, looking stiletto-sharp and with no sign of injury, Kristiansen made the break, a fast 69-second lap carrying her away from the pack. She seemed every bit her speedy old self.

Remembering Rome, they tried to catch her. Two laps later the German and the two Russians were gaining, but certainly not overtaking, when suddenly Kristiansen jolted to a stop. Wincing with pain, her right foot having truly given out, she stepped gingerly off the track and was carried away on a stretcher.

Kristiansen's unexpected departure left Kathrin Ullrich the unwilling race leader by ten metres. With no other option, the twenty-one-year-old Berliner who had won bronze at the World Championships now put on the steam, upping her lead by twenty metres.

On her tail were the two red-vested Russians. But Liz, still running her own race, was slowly but surely closing on the three of them. She passed the Russians and caught the big German just before the halfway mark of the race.

With 5200 metres to go Liz was leading, the two Russians staying in spiking distance right on her heels, Ullrich worn out and trailing.

Running from the front is the hardest way to win a race. But Liz had no intention of letting anyone past now. Knowing that she would be unable to outsprint either of the Russians to the line, for they both had better kicks than hers, she ran steadily but slightly faster on each lap. If she could make the race pace too fast for her pursuers' comfort, if she could get too far away for them to be able to make up the ground at the end, the gold would be hers. She wanted it badly.

The 10,000 is a gruelling distance to race at, and she ran the next dozen laps at a gruelling pace. It was lonely at the front of the field, even with the Russians crowding her.

With three laps left, Liz put in a 73-second lap – fast since they had already come a long way. That burned off the most dangerous of the two Russians. Yelena Zhupiyeva, the world silver medallist, dropped back and settled for Olympic bronze.

Only Olga Bondarenko followed. With the whole track available to her, Bondarenko ran in Liz's shadow, almost in Liz's vest. It was intended to be intimidating, and it was. The dark-haired, twenty-eight-year-old European silver medallist from Volgograd had a powerful physique.

Her strength, allied with that other asset, her lightness, were a dangerous combination. Bondarenko stood a mere five foot one inches and weighed in at a scant six stone six. She looked bigger. She ran bigger, too.

She had set her first world 10,000-metre record at the age of twenty-one. There were very few women who had lasted that long in the top echelon.

Liz tried to shake her off, but she couldn't go any faster and she could see that Bondarenko knew it. But it is never over until it is over. As the Russian kicked past Liz on the last lap, Liz tried first to go with her, then tried to catch her, pumping her legs and slashing the air with those pointed elbows in an effort to propel herself forward faster, but her muscles wouldn't respond. She had nothing left.

Liz had done all the work of the race, had seemed on the point of winning the Olympic gold medal, only to be cruelly demoted on the very last lap to silver.

Anderson appeared from nowhere, putting his arm around Liz's dejected shoulders. The photograph of Liz that would go round the world depicted an athlete's calvary. An Olympic silver medal, people would tell her over and over again, was something to be proud of.

'My daughter has won a silver medal,' Martin Lynch said to the media. 'That is no disgrace.'

Nor was it. It was a very great achievement.

'I ran the best race I could. I ran hard. I ran tough,' Liz said. 'I kept my head down and concentrated so hard that it could have been raining or snowing and I wouldn't have noticed. But in the end I had no answer. Bondarenko is a fine runner and deserved her win on the day.'

Bondarenko had sprinted over the line, having run the final two hundred metres in a blistering 31.2 seconds. But she did not and would not dominate distance running the way Ingrid Kristiansen had.

There would never be an Olympic medal in Kristiansen's trophy room, but the woman who stepped off the Olympic track with what turned out to be a fracture in the arch of her right foot was the greatest athlete of her generation. That sad departure by the queen of the track had left the throne vacant.

Liz would soon speak of her second place in the Olympics as the moment she had arrived as a top world contender. It was. But some part of her would regard it for ever – as Fatima had her silver at the Commonwealth Games, and Steve Backley would his bronze in Barcelona – as a great disappointment.

'I will be back,' Liz said, 'and next time it will be different. This time it's silver. Next time it will definitely be gold. I will be *harder* and more prepared.' She and her coach were intending to work on her kick.

Liz took little solace from the fact that she had finished well ahead of Zhupiyeva and Ullrich who had won silver and bronze in the World Championships. They were great runners, but insiders in athletics know how difficult it is when the Olympics are only one year later for a world champion to peak again for the Games. It almost never happens.

For weeks, even months afterward, Peter McColgan and his father-in-law would sit in front of the television watching the video of the last laps of that race over and over, frame by frame. When they went out into the gloom of a long Scottish winter to the hotel bar they both liked for a pint – one for Peter, three or more for Martin – Liz didn't go, she doesn't drink – they continued to discuss the Olympic final with consternation and grief and a growing anger.

Liz had done everything she could to win.

She had raced hard, raced well, but by the end of the race she had been so exhausted that Bondarenko had easily sprinted past. It was not Liz's fault. But someone had to be to blame.

— 11 —

The Turning Point

'Me and my son-in-law, her husband, have sat and tried to analyse
it. We've stopped the tapes, we've looked back on them. He is
more of an expert on athletics than I am. We've kenned this and
we've both come to the same conclusion.' Martin Lynch leans
forward in his armchair and reaches past the switched-off ionizer
his daughter gave him to his cigarette packet. He has been showing me videos of Liz's famous races. The sight of that whole
stadium on its feet, wildly cheering Liz home on her first great
victory at the Edinburgh Commonwealth Games had both of us
weeping. The race in Seoul moves him in a quite different way.

Betty Lynch brings in coffee and scones. Their granddaughter
Eilish, playing at her little desk beside the enormous television,
knocks my tape recorder to the floor.

Martin lights up. Exhaling, he says, 'If you go back and look
at the race you see the one pace, there was nothing there for her
to finish with, it was just plod, plod, plod, plod, one pace all the
time. Hence when Bondarenko went past her, she looked so good
and Elizabeth was just left for dead. Because that week up to the
race at the Olympics where you should have been running down
and not doing mileage, she ran something like ninety miles, which
was too much. And she reckons if she hadnae been doing that
kind of training, she would have won it.'

This is a point of great contention.

At the press conference before her departure for the Tokyo
World championships in 1991, Liz said that she had run eighty-
three miles the week of the 1988 Olympics – far too many, and
that was why she had only won silver.

John Anderson says that if Liz ran eighty-three miles that week, it was not on his advice. Before a major competition an athlete always cuts down on the miles. Every coach and every club runner knows this. This principle is well known, though the terminology varies. You 'trim' your mileage, you 'taper', you 'ease off', or, to use the parlance of the man who coached Liz at Alabama, John Mitchell, you 'point'.

Dorothy Anderson is adamant: 'She ran thirty to thirty-five miles in the week of the Olympics. John never tells you to do high mileage in the week before a race. He would have had her easing off, maybe sixty to sixty-five miles the week before that. Her regular mileage was eighty or a hundred a week. In the week of the Olympics he did not tell her to do eighty-three miles as Liz said in print. I have the training schedules.'

Yet both Peter and Martin say they have seen the mileage written down in Liz's training diary. She still keeps thorough logs of her training, as Harry taught her to do.

Could she have been running secret extra miles?

Kirsty Wade, who saw her daily at Nihon and frequently in Seoul, says, 'She used to go out in the morning. I couldn't tell you what she ran. I know she went out.'

Liz was a glutton for mileage, and still is. Harry had trouble keeping her from overdoing it. John Mitchell says, 'The tendency would be for Liz to run closer to maximum mileage weekly than for her to run closer to minimum mileage, let's put it that way.'

Shortly after the Olympics, Anderson was named coach of the year, largely because of what he and Liz had achieved at Seoul. Liz, who attended the presentation, said, 'He thoroughly deserves it. He's such a good motivator. Everything I have achieved is down to John.' She had realized that an Olympic silver was worth something. Race promoters, the men who paid appearance money, looked at her with new eyes. Rivals showed more respect.

But 'after Seoul, she had a wee downer', says Martin Lynch. Liz took a four-month break from racing, though during it she won the Scottish indoor 1500- and 3000-metre titles. She was able to spend a lot more time with Peter. Peter, who was after all an internationally ranked steeplechaser, had strong ideas about his wife's training. He did not like Anderson. When the McColgans stayed at the Andersons' house in Coventry, Peter used to sit at the table his lips pursed, wordless.

During the winter Liz put on weight. People gave up on her. Not John Anderson. Later she would say she purposely gained the extra pounds because she had been trying to get pregnant. It hadn't worked.

As usual, Liz and Anderson flew to Bali for the start of the winter road-racing season. 'I want to show that I can be a good road runner and good track runner and that you don't have to choose between the two.' There was half a million dollars on offer for a new world 10K record. Liz won the race that February – 1989 – but did not set a record. She had to make do with prize money of just $25,000.

From Bali they flew to London, where they were met by Dorothy Anderson with a change of tickets. Anderson and Liz then flew on to Tucson, Arizona, for six weeks of training. They were later joined by Dorothy and Peter. In Tucson the times Liz was running on the training track were phenomenal, and this time the line was in the right place.

'I'm in the best shape I've ever been in,' Liz said, crediting the speed training she was doing in Tucson. 'Nobody would've predicted we could go that fast that soon. I didn't realize in two weeks the speed would come on like that.'

On impulse, Liz flew to Budapest to try to break Zola Budd's world 3000-metre record at the World Indoor Championships. 'I didn't decide until the Tuesday night before that I wanted to run there. I left Arizona Wednesday, went to London, stayed overnight and then went to Budapest.'

She broke Zola's record, lowering her personal best by five seconds to 8 minutes 34.8. Unfortunately, tall, blonde Elly Van Hust of the Netherlands, who was to win gold in Barcelona, finished one second ahead of Liz and she got credited with the new world record. Liz collected another silver medal.

Twenty minutes later, after a whiff of oxygen in the ambulance they had in the stadium for emergencies – it is a good thing no one had a heart attack – Liz returned to the track for an unplanned 1500-metre outing, finishing sixth against the world's best at the distance although she herself, as a 10,000-metre specialist, was running way under-distance.

Then she flew back across the Atlantic to Orlando where she would be running in her third Red Lobster 10K Classic. She was met at the airport by the man from *Florida Running*. Over a chicken sandwich and a chocolate fudgecake sundae – like every woman, evidently, Liz sometimes went off her diet – she told him how success had changed her. For she was now established as a world-class athlete – the silver medallist at two major games. 'I'm not the little girl that was just breaking through.

'I used to be very quiet. I'm quite a shy person, really. You can't be shy any more because people think you are stand-offish, and they get the wrong impression of you. I've had to sort of force myself to be more natural and open so it's easier for people to approach me. I enjoy myself a lot more because of it. Last year, if you would have picked me up at the airport, it would have just been: "Hi, you're from Red Lobster? Take me to the hotel." Instead, we sit here eating ice cream.'

Five days later, on 11 March under sunny skies, Liz set her third consecutive world best in the road race. She had wanted to whittle the 10K record by the slimmest of margins so that it would be easier to reset in Bali where there was a half-million-dollar bonus on offer for a world record. But Kristiansen was there this time, and Liz took no chances. She ran hard from the start, winning in 30 minutes, 38 seconds, chopping twenty-one seconds off her own world record.

She had realized early in the race that she was going too fast but she hadn't realized it was that fast: 'At about a hundred metres from the line, I saw the clock and said to myself, "My God, this is too fast!" So I more or less stopped dead in my tracks. I actually walked across the finish line. That felt weird.'

The prize this time was $34,500. There is no record of the appearance money that might have been paid. Liz was to do two more lucrative road races in the States, by no means as many as she could have crammed in. She gave credit to her 'sensible coach who plans out everything for me', and who limited her races lest she burn out. Of course it was she who had decided to go to Budapest, leaving him in Tucson.

She was now a very confident twenty-four-year-old woman about to embark on a well-paid track tour of all the best places on both sides of the Atlantic. 'I know what I want in life, and I'll go after it. And I know when I'm capable of getting it or not. I just keep my feet on the ground, my head clear, and go for what I want.'

Meanwhile, she and Peter settled into a bigger house, set in three acres, with a carriage house adjoining in which Liz's parents would live. White stone Woodfield House, on to which they have built an extension, has big bay windows that let in a lot of sun. Set amid golden fields in the rolling countryside of Arbroath, the place is twenty minutes' drive from Dundee. Outside the door and down the driveway there is a network of country lanes which are perfect for a ten- or even a twenty-mile run.

There is a natural spring and a stone pond which could be a wonder of the property, but at the moment the pond is a source of consternation because it leaks. Martin Lynch was itching to repair it.

The luxurious black-tiled Jacuzzi, surrounded by plants in a room full of light, is wonderful. There's a sauna and a tiny gym which is dominated by the electric treadmill, useful for staying dry in horrid weather. Kristiansen's was in her Oslo kitchen. The treadmill, which many health clubs now also have, and which can be regulated to go as fast or as slow as you like, helps perfect the ability to run at a steady pace. Facing the treadmill is a mirror in which Liz can examine her footfalls and her stance.

That spring, 1989, the Andersons were also thinking of moving. 'We were looking for a house in Scotland in the borders.' But, says Dorothy Anderson, 'We thought that Liz was keen that we move near her. She sent cuttings from the newspaper about houses nearby. She sent the cutting of the house I'm now living in.'

Liz denies that their move had anything to do with her. She and Peter had cuttings from estate agents because they had been looking for a house too, so since the Andersons were interested, she says, she sent them on. She was not trying to inveigle them to live near her as a boon to her training.

The truth of this one we will never know.

In March of 1989 the Andersons set up a business specially, Dorothy says, to facilitate the payments Anderson was now going to receive from Liz. It was called Leisure and Recreation Consultants. Anderson had presented Liz with a five-year contract, which asked for twenty per cent of the income from the product endorsement contracts (sponsorship) and race appearance money contracts he was negotiating for her. Liz had broken with her business manager Kim McDonald when she started with Anderson in 1986. Since then, he had been her manager as well as coach.

'John received no payment until March, eighty-nine,' says Dorothy. 'I know because I did the accounts.'

The dean of athletics correspondents, the *Guardian*'s conservative John Rodda, reported that this was indeed the fact. 'He began coaching McColgan after her disastrous performance at the European Championships in 1986, but only received payment for coaching and managing her programme three years later.' During her time with Anderson, Rodda said, McColgan earned £280,000 in prize money and endorsements. The man from the *Glasgow Herald* put the figure a little lower, at £250,000.

'I saw the contract that he drew up,' says Martin Lynch. 'Who gets twenty per cent? Say, for example, if she won a car, she was to sell the car and give him half the money.'

Vi Bennett had said there was a car Liz won that Anderson had wanted, and Liz had told him that if she was going to give a car away she had a brother she could give it to. Was the story true?

'Aye. That was in the contract, you sell the car he gets fifty per cent.'

Liz never signed the contract. But you don't have to sign a contract in Scottish law. It is binding if you agree to it verbally. Liz says she didn't. Anderson says she did.

'It's word against word,' sighs Martin.

'He'd seen the potential, he kenned where she was gonna go, he knew what she was gonna do.'

'He didn't see her as a moneybags,' says Dorothy Anderson. 'John does a lot for free.'

'We're not mercenary,' says Anderson. 'I have young athletes here to stay all the time. We feed them, train them, lend them the car. Liz and Peter stayed here with us.'

Allegedly the contract which Anderson presented to Liz but she never signed, but which seems to have gone into operation – he was now getting paid – gives Anderson twenty per cent of everything.

The percentage is by no means outrageous in the world of sport where the major agencies sometimes take twenty-five per cent or more. Allan Pascoe Associates, which negotiates endorsements for the British Olympic athletic team as a whole, would, I was told, take 17½ per cent from a client like Liz.

After the wonderful winter of successes, Liz had a disappointing summer season on the track. Perhaps the new house plus the new arrangement with her coach added up to too much distraction. Unused to being defeated, Liz had, says her father, 'another wee downer'. She took another break.

'I took two and a half months off because I had completely lost my appetite. I lost all my aggression.' When during the lay-off she put on weight, many gave up on her ever finding form again. But as she left with the Andersons for the Commonwealth Games in November of 1989 Liz said, 'I'm hungry to race again.'

She would be away for nearly three months. Peter was left at home. The Games were in New Zealand, but the British team's holding camp was at the Australian Institute of Sport in Canberra. After eleven weeks there, Liz would go on to the Games in Auckland, New Zealand, where she was defending her 10,000-metre Commonwealth crown and hoping to pick up the 3000 metres.

Liz was in good spirits in Canberra, very friendly with everyone. This holding camp was far better than Nihon, not so hilly, and there were lots of runs. Also, compared to the Olympics these Games would be a doddle.

There was time to make new private friendships or go ten-pin bowling with the group. 'Liz was very good at it,' says Dorothy Anderson, 'so she was the centre of attention. She seemed fine, very sociable, in a good mood.'

In the Mount Smart Stadium in Auckland Liz retained her 10,000-metre Commonwealth crown, running a fast final

Right Liz's husband Peter is now her official coach. *(Gray Mortimore/Allsport)*

Below To attain her dream of being the greatest distance runner ever, Liz has already come a long way – much of it on Scottish country lanes. *(Gray Mortimore/Allsport)*

The winner of the lauded and lucrative New York Marathon soon finds the streets paved with gold. *(Mike Powell/Allsport)*

Asked to kiss the winner of the men's Marathon, the number one woman pointed out she had never met him – so number one man Salvador Garcia of Mexico kissed Liz. *(Associated Press)*

The McColgan family, Liz, Eilish and Peter, in front of their elegant white house in Arbroath. *(Syndication International)*

Above right Pleased and proud to be BBC Sports Personality of the Year, 1991. *(Syndication International)*

Below right Crowning a miraculous year: Michael Aspel announces to an astonished Liz, 'This is Your Life.' *(D. C. Thomson Ltd)*

Yvonne Murray on Liz's shoulder in the 1992 race at Meadowbank that buried their grudge. *(Gray Mortimore/Allsport)*

No tea party in Boston. At the 1992 world cross-country championships, snow, a virus and over-training united to defeat her. *(Mike Powell/Allsport)*

Above Liz leading the pack, with Elana Meyer and Derartu Tulu close on her heels, in the middle stages of the Barcelona Olympic final. *(Mike Powell/Allsport)*

Below Liz's Olympic defeat became a victory for African unity when gold medallist Derartu Tulu of Ethiopia joined hands with South African Elana Meyer, the silver medallist. *(Mike Powell/Allsport)*

67-second lap. It was a good way to start the 1990s. At home in Arbroath Peter watched the race, which started at 6.10 a.m. British time, on television. 'I set the alarm but I didn't need it. I was wide awake long before it went off.'

After the race he spoke to Liz on the phone. 'She said she'd felt really confident right throughout – that it felt real easy.'

She also won the 3000. 'I hope this will have silenced my critics,' Liz said. 'Last year I suddenly went from being Scotland's golden girl to Scotland's no-hoper. They said some stupid things.' Particularly about her weight. When she finally got home, with her two gold medals, there would be another homecoming celebration through the streets of Dundee.

But first Liz and Anderson were going to Java where Liz had won the race, normally held in Bali, twice in the last three years. The prize on offer, not counting any appearance money, was $20,000 with a big bonus for a world record.

Shortly before the flight, Liz said she wasn't going.

'But we have a contract,' Anderson said.

Liz told him she thought she might be coming down with a virus.

'But it's all arranged,' Anderson said. Conceivably there was time to get over the virus – if it was one.

Liz made it very clear that she was going home. But if they didn't go to Java, not only would she get a reputation as a no-show, so would Anderson. Without Liz competing the meeting would be badly crippled. The promoters would be livid with rage, and neither Anderson nor Liz would receive any money.

'If you agree a contract, you keep it,' Dorothy Anderson says her husband told Liz. But there was no convincing her.

'She changes her mind just like that,' says Dorothy Anderson. 'John never argued with her. Liz dictated and ruled all the way.'

But what about the virus? Remember that Liz willingly ran with a virus – a cold sore and a sore throat – at the 1992 World Cross-country Championships – where Peter was coach and everything was all arranged.

'She could have run in Java despite the infection,' Peter told the local paper, 'but because she didn't feel a hundred per cent and because she's been away from home so long she decided to just come home. Those people who say that she just runs for the money should now see that this certainly isn't the case.'

The *Dundee Courier & Advertiser*, whose source was Peter and her parents, reported that Liz had a urinary infection.

Arriving home, according to the *Courier*, on 5 February, a week early, Liz said, 'A few of the athletes picked up some sort of virus in Auckland. I was put on antibiotics and advised by doctors to take things easy for a couple of days.'

The climate made Java a very hard race unless you were feeling perfectly fit.

The next problem was how to get home. The promoter had agreed to pay their fares to the Philippines and Java and then home to the UK. If they didn't go to the race Anderson and Liz were stranded in New Zealand without a ticket home. Dorothy Anderson says her husband at last laid down the law. He was not a rich man. She was quite a well-to-do young lady.

'If you are not going,' Anderson told Liz, 'you are going to have to pay for your own air ticket home, and for mine.' *The Times* had reported that his and his wife's expenses at the games were already costing £4500, a lot to them.

Having no choice, Liz dug deep in her pockets and bought the tickets. It didn't take a mind reader to realize she was not pleased.

It occurred to her then, and not for the first time, that she should end her relationship with John Anderson.

'She told me in Australia that she had had it with John Anderson,' one of the PR men who knows her well says.

'Why?'

He rolls his eyes.

'Well?'

'There were a lot of factors. One of them, though, was she wanted someone who would charge a smaller percentage.'

Liz didn't like the idea of making John Anderson rich even if it was making her richer. It was now only a matter of time before they parted.

It didn't seem that way to the Andersons. There had often been clashes. There was no reason, it seemed to them, to think that a little quarrel over an air ticket might be terminal. Anderson took early retirement from his job as Southwark recreation officer in

London, and Dorothy and John Anderson made an offer on a house about an hour's drive from the McColgans.

After Auckland, Liz had another 'wee downer'. This time she had been victorious, so disappointment on the track was not the reason. When she got home, Liz concentrated on Peter.

'At the Commonwealth Games I was away from Peter for three months – it wasn't right. Now I'll have him around me to give me help and support when I need it.' Soon she discovered she was pregnant.

She rang the Andersons in Coventry to tell them. Dorothy answered the telephone. John was in America.

Dorothy Anderson remembers that Liz told her she was ten weeks pregnant. 'I don't know what John will say,' Dorothy remembers Liz saying.

'He'll be thrilled.'

But Liz seemed worried. She and Anderson had been planning great things for the coming year. The pregnancy would, of course, disrupt her running.

Dorothy reassured her: 'He'll be very pleased for you, Liz.' She rang her husband in America and told him. 'He rang Liz straight away from America to tell her he was delighted for her.'

The Andersons saw Liz in July. Liz was happy to be pregnant, but on a day-to-day basis she was finding it trying. For an athlete of Liz's standard, feeling physically under par for weeks on end was difficult. It is not surprising that to Dorothy Anderson Liz 'seemed miserable, she was pouty, short-tempered'.

Also in July one of Anderson's other runners, Yobes Ondieki, broke with him. Their parting was not sweet sorrow. Anderson had been coaching the Kenyan for just five months. On his own, Ondieki had reached the Olympic 5000-metre final and become the first man in a decade to beat Aouita. Then nothing more had happened. When he and Anderson joined forces in Auckland, the sport's insiders got excited. 'Everyone speculated,' says Duncan Mackay of *Athletics Today*, 'that Ondieki's talent allied with Anderson's technical ability might produce a new world 5000-metre record.'

But Ondieki wasn't winning races. He blamed his poor early

season results on over-training. 'John worked me so hard that I couldn't even finish a slow twenty-minute jog,' said Ondieki. He had had trouble with a previous coach. 'Now I'm coaching myself and I'll have only myself to blame if I run badly.'

Those who knew about training felt Ondieki's better results as the season progressed were due to Anderson. 'His improved performances probably resulted from Anderson's more structured approach to training that has emphasized speed endurance and better race judgement,' wrote Mackay. 'Athletes looking after themselves usually fail to make much impact at major championships. Self-coached Olympic champions are few and far between.'

Anderson, who was widely regarded as Britain's finest multi-event coach, had been unhappy to read about the split in the newspapers. He told *The Scotsman* that it was he who was leaving Ondieki because his attitude 'was not appropriate to the coach–athlete relationship'.

In August Liz rang the Andersons, reaching them at their new cottage in Scotland. 'We were in the house for the weekend doing some things to get it ready,' says Dorothy. 'We were moving in the following month. Liz rang and said to John, "I don't want you to coach me any more."'

Anderson was amazed and astonished. He was also angry and hurt. 'You can't do that, Liz, you have a contract,' he finally said.

But Liz had never signed the contract and did not believe she had accepted it verbally. Anderson believed she had done so. He hung up the telephone unsure what to do.

Liz was appointing her husband Peter coach. Of Anderson she said, 'I don't think he is suitable to my needs any more.' She had decided to pursue different training methods.

That was 'nonsense', said Anderson. He would be taking advice on the matter. The following year, on 1 May 1991, Anderson filed suit for breach of contract. It was the first time a coach had ever sued an athlete.

'Since Mrs McColgan's actions left me only the choice of accepting her decision, or challenging it through a legal procedure, I have taken the latter course of action,' he said.

On 17 May, Liz issued a statement: 'Between October 1986

and August 1990 when John Anderson was my coach, he received twenty per cent of athletics earnings negotiated by him, plus expenses for warm-weather training and preparing for the 1990 Commonwealth Games. This amount has been paid in full.

'I have never been involved in any contractual agreement with Mr Anderson, and was not the reason he took early retirement and returned to reside in Scotland.

'I am no longer associated with Mr Anderson and am under no obligation to him.'

One question on which the lawsuit, which both parties hoped would be settled out of court, would be waged was whether or not she had accepted the contract verbally. The case, already postponed once, is supposed to reach court in December 1992.

The divorce of coach and athlete and the subsequent lawsuit brought a lot of anger to the surface. By September 1991, when Liz departed for the World Championships, it was near boiling point. By bringing up the issue of the mileage in Seoul, Liz fanned the flames.

It is likely that news of Ondieki's rift with Anderson had triggered or helped trigger Liz's phone call breaking it off with Anderson. It may also be the genesis of what appears to have been an inadvertent lapse of memory.

In the weeks before the Olympics Anderson's training schedule may have been tiring for Liz. Before her departure for the Nihon holding camp, three and a half weeks before the Seoul final, Liz McColgan had spoken of fatigue, which was all part of the grand plan. 'I got a bit tired because I was running hard every day, but we did that on purpose because it was the last week's training,' she told *The Times*. Liz is referring to the last week before her departure for the camp, not the last week before the Olympics. 'The routine in Seoul is lot lighter, and I hope the effect will be to rest me up so that I can run well.'

The summer training had consisted of very high mileage and thrice weekly sessions on the track with the emphasis on strength rather than speed. The speed work which Anderson had introduced into her training and they had worked so hard on the previous year would again become a priority in Nihon. Could it be that over the years the weeks merged in Liz's memory?

The prospect of renegotiating her Nike shoe company endorsement contract was also a factor. They made her an offer she could well refuse – and was angered by – reputed to be just twenty per cent of what she had been getting. Their rationale may have been that she was not very marketable. She was not winning races, not even running in them (she was pregnant) and not likely to run again. In Britain few new mothers returned to the track to become great champions and – this was crucial – she preferred training to turning up for publicity events.

Liz did not re-sign with Nike.

During the time she was pregnant, during 1990, she wasn't earning. It was only natural that she would have wanted to watch every penny. She would not have wanted to give Anderson a slice of what was a very small pie or what she hoped in the future would be a golden layer cake. Money was a big factor in the split with Anderson.

The personality clash seems to have been another. Said one Dundonian who is fond of both of them, 'They were two of a kind. Both of them given to speaking their mind, both of them fighters. Of course eventually they had to clash.'

Peter, and what role he would have in Liz's life, was perhaps the key. Not only did he have strong views on training, he had also worked for the Inland Revenue and knew a thing or two about contracts and percentages. In the rift with Anderson, Peter was by no means an insignificant factor.

'Let's face it,' Martin Lynch says, 'there was a young lassie and young fella got married, they wanted their own way and I think they were right.'

It is over a decade since David Moorcroft's great days on the track, but the retired athlete and his former coach remain close. David Bedford was protectively wary when I asked him about Anderson, whom he described as 'my good friend'. Anderson has maintained a good relationship with many of his ex-athletes. In the summer of Barcelona he stayed overnight at David Moorcroft's house. Moorcroft's daughter is his godchild. But when it is over with Anderson, it's all over.

In his column in *Athletics Today* Anderson would write of

Ondieki that 'being a great runner does not necessarily qualify an athlete as a great human being'.

On the eve of the Seoul Olympics, he had said of Liz, 'Not only is she a brilliant and dedicated runner, she is good looking, slim and has a fantastic personality. The combination makes her very marketable.'

Since Anderson undertook legal proceedings, each side's view of the other has become more entrenched and pointed. Family members on both sides are full of venom which they can't help themselves from voicing. Whenever the subject is mentioned, the anger level goes through the roof.

Quite properly, neither Anderson nor Liz will discuss the legal case. Anderson told me he would not discuss the contract he put before his star athlete, that he would discuss training but not money, and he didn't stray beyond the limits he had set during any of our interviews, not on the telephone, not on the train ride from London to Sheffield, or during the long talk in his hotel room in Sheffield.

Anderson's new protégée is Katharine Merry, the seventeen-year-old junior sprinter who beat Sally Gunnell a week after Gunnell won gold in Barcelona. Anderson has been coaching her for some time. He thinks she is going places and will arrive in 1996.

In Sheffield, in the summer of 1992, Katharine Merry's family took the Andersons out for a meal. Liz, who was earning thousands and thousands of pounds a year and often ate at their table, says Dorothy, never did.

'John has a contract with Katharine Merry, but there has been no money yet. It has actually cost him to set up the contract. She comes to stay. Katharine Merry's mother offers housekeeping money but none of the other athletes pay – I often have a house full of athletes – why should she?'

In a television interview Liz said recently that she didn't think coaches should be paid. In the old days they weren't paid, but neither were the athletes. There is something skew about the notion that a coach at the very top of his profession who works hard and helps an athlete earn a million pounds should get nothing but his travelling expenses. A few coaches get money but it isn't usually talked about. This is the new shamateurism. It too must go. Since the start of the law case, this has become an issue of the moment. People at high levels in British sport, not just in athletics, are waiting to see what happens.

Meanwhile John and Dorothy Anderson are not just angry, they also feel hurt. 'Liz's Olympic silver and her world record are part of his achievement as a coach,' says Dorothy. 'It was good coaching. He is a very respected coach, one of the best in the country. She did 4.1 with John. In Sheffield, in the build-up to the Barcelona Olympics, it was only 4.16.

'But Liz is hurting John. He is upset about it. He would have loved to carry on. There was no clash, no argument. I don't know why they parted.' Dorothy says. 'Liz has said it was the wrong sort of coaching.' Dorothy Anderson cannot accept this.

The McColgans have this same ambivalence. They know John Anderson was an important part of their lives. They want to forget him, but not to be forgotten by him. I was baffled at first when Peter McColgan told me, very heatedly, 'John Anderson is planning to leave Liz out of his autobiography.' Peter sounded angry and hurt.

I soon found out that John Anderson's lengthy memoirs run to 120,000 words (nearly twice the length of this book). Written with the help of Yvonne Murray's ex-fiancé, the experienced journalist and PR man Nigel Whitefield, the memoirs were originally to have focused on Anderson's most illustrious successes: Daley Thompson, whom he advised for a time, David Bedford, David Moorcroft and Liz. At the moment, says Whitefield, the book is on ice.

Dorothy Anderson, as you may remember, is a physiotherapist. In her treatment room, which becomes the dining room when she and John have a lot of people over, there are three framed photographs. One is of John Anderson and the great David Moorcroft, one is of John and his young sprinter Katharine Merry, the third is of John with Liz.

'John hasn't taken the photograph down, a fact which amazes me,' Dorothy Anderson says. 'I said to him, "Don't you want to take it down, John?" He didn't.'

— 12 —

The Crown Princess

Miriam Stoppard's book on childbirth had become almost as familiar an item to Liz as her trainers. She was having a very easy pregnancy but she was eager now for the baby to be born. Her weight had shot up beyond ten stone – two and a half stone more than usual. For her five feet and nearly seven inches it was not that heavy, but to Liz it must have felt mountainous. She had been delighted to be pregnant; now in the last months of 1990, as she neared term, she would be equally delighted to be delivered of the child. 'The baby's had enough of my body for now. Its time is up – I want to get back to my running.'

After the first weeks home from Auckland, Liz had felt oddly out of breath when she was training. It was, she says, 'like running at altitude'. She was a bit overweight too. A visit to the doctor had revealed she was pregnant.

Once she knew the cause Liz ignored the breathlessness, training as usual for the first three months. 'I ran eighty-five to ninety miles a week.' From three to seven months she put in five miles a day, six days a week. Sometimes the pace was very fast. 'I've been listening to what my body's been telling me. One day when I was around six months pregnant, I felt really good and I ran my five-mile loop in thirty-one minutes.'

In her eighth month, Liz, now twenty-six, was running three miles every second day. 'At that stage I was getting uncomfortable, and I was getting sore quads with the weight of the baby.'

Unlike the Olympic champion from Georgia, the sprinter Gwen Torrence, who had been virtually bedridden for three months when she was pregnant the year before, Liz was having no trouble. 'I haven't had any sickness or heartburn either and I think it's all due to just being really healthy.'

Actually, it was the luck of the draw. Torrence, who like Liz would be gunning for gold at the World Championships, was healthy but ill. And Ingrid Kristiansen had a very easy first pregnancy and a difficult second one.

With her first baby, Kristiansen hadn't even realized she was pregnant until she was in her fifth month. Because she was virtually all skin and bones, like Liz and many other top athletes, she had temporarily stopped having periods.

Amenorrhoea is par for the course. In women who train hard and have very little body fat, ovulation ceases, hormone production slows and bones begin to thin at about the rate of a post-menopausal woman.

Everything gets back to normal when the runner cuts down a bit on training and eats more so that her body fat increases to the percentage of her body weight that nature deems suitable for nurturing babies. Then, like any other woman, all other things being equal, if she wants to she can become pregnant.

Liz knew all of this, of course, but secretly she had been worried that she couldn't have children. Both she and Peter told the media about her fear and what a relief it had been to learn she was pregnant. She was looking forward to indulging her forbidden lust for chocolate.

Instead her pre-natal cravings turned out to be for grapes and bananas, which she says she ate 'all day and all night'. She felt fat having put on all that weight, but if you hadn't known her before she didn't look fat. The baby, who was due on 12 November, took her time arriving.

The family squeezed into Liz's quarter of the four-bed hospital room where Liz looked plump for her and tired, and Peter as ecstatic as an athlete who has just won Olympic gold. Flowers poured in, followed by so many photographers that Liz was soon moved to a private room. She had her baby after a forty-eight-hour labour at Ninewells, the same hospital Karen had gone to for her lung operation.

None of the photographers got even a glimpse of baby Eilish.

Liz was determined to keep them away, and there were no photographs published of the baby for months after her birth on 25 November 1990.

'Eilish has nothing to do with my running world. So my husband Peter and I decided to keep her private. We don't want to put any pressure on her while she's so young.'

'Then she had to show them,' says Betty Lynch, 'because they thought something was wrong with the baby.' At four months old, Eilish made her first brief TV appearance.

'The only reason I've allowed her to be on TV,' her mother said, 'was just to show that we weren't hiding her because she had two heads or anything like that.'

Fair, wispy-haired Eilish is now a lively, energetic toddler. They say that with her blazing blue eyes she looks exactly like her daddy.

'The only thing she has like me,' Liz has said, 'is big feet and long legs.' Liz once jokingly allowed that the baby was hyperkinetic like her mother. Actually, she's perfect, as I now say to Betty Lynch.

'Aye.'

For a long time Liz didn't talk about the baby in public either, so some people erroneously concluded she had had Eilish for professional reasons. Whenever a runner gets pregnant, people suspect she is having the baby to improve her running. Runners have their babies for the same reasons other women do, but because pregnancy is nature's own endurance training they get the perk of a training boost. As a result, they also get trouble from the media.

America's then sweetheart Mary Decker Slaney had a glorious 1985 season on the track, then sat out most of the next season pregnant. Asked by a hostile *Times* man if she had got pregnant because she thought it would improve her running, Slaney said that was *one* of the reasons. She saw no shame in it. Nor should she. Like Liz and Ingrid Kristiansen, like Gwen Torrence and many, many others, Slaney was also at the age and in the circumstances of life when many women decide to have children. But in sporting circles it has been common knowledge for over a decade that mothers run best.

This was not always the case. In bomb-scarred London at the 1948 Olympics, the Dutchwoman Fanny Blankers-Koen huddled out of the rain under the umbrella that Jan, her coach and latterly also her husband, held over her and waited for her race to begin. She was thirty, which was thought to be past it and, as the papers put it, 'the blonde-haired mother of two'. Motherhood it was thought had worn her out. A top British coach had publicly chided her. At the Games Blankers-Koen, the woman with the most to prove, won four gold medals.

The *London Daily Graphic* reported Fanny Blankers-Koen's great victory, her second Olympic gold medal, like this: 'FASTEST WOMAN IN THE WORLD IS AN EXPERT COOK.' No one was denying her achievement, double Olympic gold. But the newspaper headline and article stressed her traditionally feminine roles. 'I shall train my two children to be athletes as well,' said a smaller boldface headline. The article continued: 'But at home she is just an ordinary housewife. She is an expert cook and darns socks with artistry. *Her greatest love next to racing is housework.*' (My italics.) I've never met anyone who *loved* it.

Fanny Blankers-Koen was the first of the famous mothers who run. The roster of champion mother-athletes is large, and it continues to grow. In Blankers-Koen's day it was thought that having a baby was a liability to a runner. No more.

'I've heard that childbirth makes women stronger with a quicker recovery [rate],' Liz said while pregnant. 'If that's true I'll be on cloud nine. I don't think it's like a wonder drug though, you still have to work.'

Sport scientists are still not quite sure why there is a post-natal peak in performance. There seem to be biological and psychological reasons. Pregnancy has the same effect as blood-doping. Suddenly there are more blood vessels which can feed more than the normal amount of oxygen to the muscles, and this is very useful to a distance runner.

Some scientists think that pregnancy makes women more resistant to pain and fatigue. And it gradually conditions the heart and lungs as it forces them to become more efficient to cope with extra body weight. Liz, who nature supplied with the ideal body shape, has through training developed a larger than normal heart.

Couple that with pregnancy, which the British sports physiologist Craig Sharp calls 'nature's own aerobic conditioner', and you certainly have a winner.

Four months after Eilish was born Liz said, 'All I know is that I'm feeling stronger.'

Kristiansen's coach noticed that after the birth of her son Gaute, her first child, in 1984, her gait changed. A pelvis widened by childbirth may have contributed to a more efficient stride.

Much of the benefit, however, in Liz's and Kristiansen's case, as in others, is psychological. Once an athlete has demonstrated that she is a 'real woman', says the sports psychologist Dorothy Harris, she is likely to have fewer conflicts about excelling in sport because she no longer feels her femininity is put on the line by success.

Instead of the foolish old worries that sport might imperil the female reproductive system, the evidence shows that having a baby can – for physiological and psychological reasons – enhance a woman champion's sport. But only if she keeps training.

Liz, Kristiansen and Gwen Torrence all had support systems, families who helped with childcare, otherwise they couldn't have returned to full-time running. Betty and Martin Lynch adore looking after Eilish, and it is often her mother or Peter who gets up to see to the child in the middle of the night.

Torrence's mother looks after Mekhail when Torrence works out and when competition takes her and her husband away his parents look after the baby. Although Torrence, whose son was born a year before Liz had Eilish, didn't find she was stronger, she had become more motivated. 'The will to train was intense. You miss the sport, and you want to get back quickly, so you train hard.'

Torrence had her first post-natal run on Christmas Day 1989, a month after her delivery. 'I was barely moving. I thought I had gone out on a twenty-minute run, but by the time I got home it was only eight minutes. I had to learn to run all over.' She won no races at all in 1990. By 1991, though, she was on song. One reason her comeback took so long was that she had been too ill to train during the pregnancy.

Liz had been more fortunate, but she did not get off scot-free either. Expecting an easy delivery, she had a long labour and a difficult birth. Ordinarily, fit women have the easiest time. Stomach muscles should assist with the birth but hers, she says, were too strong. And Liz's need to control, one of the traits that makes her a great champion, could only have made it hard for her to give in to the abandon of second-stage labour.

On the eleventh day after giving birth to her blue-eyed daughter, Liz was out training on the roads. After the agony and the ecstasy of the delivery, the running was turning out to be all agony. Normally three miles was nothing to Liz, who has been known to run four just to keep her muscles loose between races.

Any woman who has ever gone out for a run, even a little jog, knows how heavy breasts can feel, how nipples chafe, but how many keep running? Her father says Liz's breasts, swollen with milk, hurt terribly. She kept on. And it wasn't just her breasts that hurt. But at a time when many women can barely walk, Liz kept running.

Giving birth, the worst pain she had ever felt, had made her able to withstand more of it in training. Liz was the sort who scowled back at any adversity.

Her first coach, Harry Bennett, had been almost exactly the same. Harry hadn't let pain stop him from running. Harry didn't ignore the pain, though. Rather, he kept an eye on it. Measured it. Checking his watch after his every run. 'I was able to run further this time before the pain came,' he had said, looking at the second hand on his stop watch. Harry Bennett insisted on living life his own way, and to him running was an essential part of it even if it meant risking dying.

Liz always did things her way, too.

Now that she had Eilish, and had conquered the fear that she could never give birth, she wanted to be the finest distance runner in the world, to be at the acme of her profession, to be the queen of the track. It would be glorious and it would be golden, surely worth a million pounds to the family bank account which was emptier than usual.

Day by day, pain or no pain, Liz upped the mileage, her head down and her sights set on the World Championships in Tokyo, where the throne was awaiting an occupant. A week before Christmas Liz had her first session on the track.

'I've been training with her for the last five or six weeks and every week she gets stronger and stronger,' Peter said. 'She didn't do anything for the first week, and her second week back was steady running. She was quickly back to seventy miles a week. We asked people like Kirsty Wade, who had had a baby' (the year before) 'and our local doctor and they said, "Really, it's up to you."'

He was astounded at her vitality.

Liz was a woman who never failed to amaze her husband. That had been evident when, at a time she was fit and in full flight, he described the routine his wife followed. 'As soon as she's up she's gone out the door within two minutes. She does everything on the stretch of the road from the house. A lot of mornings I'll run through the park for a change. Liz never does that. She does the same route every day. She says it doesn't matter because she rarely looks round or notices anything. She keeps her head down.

'She times everything. There's a pillar at the gate and she starts her watch there. She got a distance measuring wheel from the local council and painted marks on the road at 150, 300, 600, 800, 1000 metres.

'The rain washed them off, so she's put plastic bags on the fences now. Beyond a thousand metres we went round in the car to see where we could find landmarks, we went back with the wheel to be exact.

'I don't know which landmark she uses for the first mile, but I do know it's not at 1600 metres, it's at 1609, which is exactly a mile.

'She looks at her watch all the time. She trains every day in all weathers, she trains hard. That's why I say I just can't understand her. I would love to be like that. I've never met anybody like her.'

Just 119 days after Eilish's birth, Liz won a bronze medal at the World Cross-country Championships in Antwerp. The previous year she had won silver, but it was Britain's only medal and a phenomenal comeback.

The American Lynn Jennings, taking the title for the second time in a row, said of Liz who had forced the pace, 'I can't believe she only had a baby four months ago. She's fantastic and deserves a gold medal for what she did.'

A young Ethiopian called Derartu Tulu, of whom we will be hearing more later, took the silver.

But Liz was content. 'I let the world know that I am nearly back in a hundred per cent shape.'

Only Kristiansen had done as well. Five months after her first child was born, Ingrid Kristiansen won the Houston Marathon, slicing two minutes off her marathon time. Five months later she lowered her time at the London Marathon to two hours 24.26 minutes, which was a European best.

Liz's answer to that, she hoped, would be victory at the one event that ranked with the Olympics in prestige, the World Athletics Championships. Her summer season was magnificent, the only defeat one to Yvonne Murray whose tactics infuriated Liz.

'She was clipping my heels with her spikes all the time and running right against my shoulder so that there was no room for my hand to move back. I could understand it if there were seventeen people in a bunch, but there were only the two of us,' Liz was quoted as saying in the newspapers.

This, some observed, was the rough and tumble of top-level athletics; and indeed, their meeting the following year at Meadowbank was to put this incident into perspective.

Throughout that spring and summer Liz had more trouble with officialdom than with her rivals. She was at war with Frank Dick, also a Scot, who was Britain's director of coaching. When Liz declined a place in the British team for the European Cup in Frankfurt in June – on the grounds that a 10,000-metre race in June wouldn't suit her preparations for the World Championships in Tokyo – Dick proposed that she and any other athlete who turned down selection for a team event should be barred from the next major competition.

In other words, he wanted Liz off the team for Tokyo. 'What I want to have clearly established is that when the nation needs you, you shouldn't walk away,' said Dick.

'I won't be blackmailed, whatever the consequences,' Liz said over the telephone from Florida where she was in the midst of spring training. She had said she would run the 3000 in Frankfurt if they wanted her to, but 'I have no intention of running the ten thousand. I think it's a stupid proposal. I want to be at my best in Tokyo, and as I'm the best judge, I will prepare in the way I feel fit.'

The fracas with Frank Dick took place in April. Two months later, his proposal politely ignored by the British Amateur Athletics Board (BAAB), which would have had to enact it, Frank Dick named his Tokyo team. Liz was on it.

Dick was rather bemused when told by the *Times* man that Liz was now planning to run a 10,000 in June, in Holland, four days before the European Cup. Could it be a matter of appearance money?

Liz had an answer that had nothing to do with appearance money. The Dutch race, in Hengelo, would be fast, led by a hired pace-maker. Such a race would benefit her preparation for Tokyo far more than a tactical one in Frankfurt.

In Hengelo, seven months after giving birth, she won in 30 minutes 57.07 seconds, establishing herself as definite favourite to win the World Championship. Prior to that she had been third in the all-time rankings. Liz now moved up to second, ahead of Olga Bondarenko. Ingrid still held the five-year-old world record of 30 minutes 13.74 seconds. She couldn't run that fast now.

Meanwhile, Liz was locking horns with ex-police sergeant Andy Norman, the promotions officer of the British Board and still one of the most powerful men in athletics. Norman, who was the paymaster, was warning top stars that they would get a pay cut if the seats in the stadiums didn't start filling up.

Top stars like Roger Black, Chris Akabusi and Linford Christie were being paid a 'subvention' – appearance money that went into their trust funds – of between £7000 and £10,000 a race. Liz was in there somewhere, but exactly where neither Norman nor she would say.

'Subvention deals are a private matter between the athlete and the sport,' he said. 'They are based on market values, and if the market drops so does the subvention. It's as simple as that.'

Liz was irate at the idea of a pay cut. 'It's not my job to sell tickets off the track, it's up to me to do my best on it. Unless you buy a running magazine, it's difficult to find out any information about a particular meeting. The BAAB should be doing a lot more to bring in the man and woman from the street, rather than hitting out at the athletes in a pre-Olympic year.'

There was also trouble in Dundee. For some years she had been having a love–hate relationship with her native city. There were little things at first. The year after her first Commonwealth victory Liz didn't turn up at Caird Park, although she had accepted the invitation to present trophies at the Scottish University Championship. Worse, fifteen minutes later she arrived at the track for her regular training session.

Martin Lynch said it was his fault. He had forgotten to enter the date in her diary. But all was not forgiven. People still talk about that slight in Dundee.

In the *Radio Times* that same summer of 1987, Liz said she had left Dundee for college in America because she had been 'at a dead end in a dead-end town'. The council was outraged, particularly as they had recently created a full-time, £9834-a-year job for her as a sports development officer. This job was to be a bone of contention for years, and in the summer of 1991 the Tory councillors argued vociferously that it should be rescinded.

By then the contract being offered was £12,000 for a thirty-hour a *month* sports consultancy, requiring her to work with beginners and to compete in and help organize one event a year. By then, most Dundonians had heard that Liz was earning in the vicinity of £100,000 a year from running, and there was a lot of anger in Dundee where a family of five could live very well on £12,000 and unemployment was high. A year later the taxi drivers still had a lot to say on the subject.

At the Gateshead press conference on the eve of her departure for Tokyo, Liz wore her Nike sweatshirt inside out. As she wasn't getting sponsorship from them, she had been appearing at races with their name taped over on her kit and shoes.

Now, with no false modesty, she announced to the press that she would win gold in Tokyo. The World Championships, as they all knew, were the only track event which vied with the Olympics in importance.

And so she departed on her quest, confident but greatly displeased that her baby Eilish wasn't accompanying her and her husband to Tokyo. 'I'm very annoyed that I can't take her. She's been all over the world with me. I asked ages ago if the British Board could arrange some sort of creche facility. They were going to do something about it but nothing ever happened.'

A summer of aggro might not seem to be the best build-up to the race of her life, but Liz appears to thrive on controversy. Her answer to the disgrace and disappointment of Alabama had been her great 1986 Commonwealth victory in Edinburgh. Now, besieged on all sides, would she come home at the top of the world?

— 13 —

On Top of the World

There had been many doubters when Liz told the chaps she would win the world championship. She said it again to the pressmen seeing her off at Edinburgh airport. In Tokyo, she got down to business. First order of business was the semi-final which she felt confident enough to run in trainers instead of spikes. Trainers would be slower but easier on her legs, which she wanted tiptop on the day of the final. Anything to forestall the blisters of Rome.

At the eleventh hour, Kristiansen, now thirty-five, decided to make a last stand. It was a year since the birth of her second child Marte, a daughter. It was only nine months since Liz had borne Eilish.

But Kristiansen's had been a miserable pregnancy, which sometimes disrupted her training. This spring she had run the Boston Marathon which she had won in the past. She finished sixth, in her slowest time for seven years.

Now, in Tokyo, Liz husbanded her energy and finished third in the semi-final, behind Kristiansen who'd wanted to win it but was out-sprinted over the last two hundred metres by a little-known Ethiopian called Derartu Tulu. This was the same Tulu who had pipped Liz for silver at the World Cross-country in March. Under five feet tall and just nineteen, Tulu supposedly wasn't even a full-time athlete. She was listed as a prison administrator in Addis Ababa, attending high school at night. Her running club consisted entirely of prison administrators.

But no one was seriously worried about Tulu as a threat in the final. The qualifying rounds were a special case, as Britain's highly experienced director of coaching Frank Dick could tell you: '*No one* can be taken for granted in the qualifying rounds. There are a few "rabbits" out there for whom getting through a first round is like winning the gold – and they compete like it's a matter of life and death!'

Derartu Tulu appeared to be just such a rabbit. Her victory in the semi set a new Ethiopian record for the distance, but had no importance at all in the worldwide scheme of things. It was thought that, metaphorically speaking, the semi would be Derartu Tulu's only moment in the sun.

Tulu herself didn't seem to think so. Was she trying to psych them all out or speaking with uncommonly earnest honesty – who could know? – when she insisted after her victory over the world record holder, 'I was not tired. I was eager to go with Kristiansen because I knew she was a world-class runner. I was happy when I beat her.'

Well, yes. Who wouldn't be?

Tulu had wisely been modest about her chances in the final. 'It won't be easy because there are many good runners.' Fifteen finalists, of whom the *Tokyo Daily Yomiuri* listed Liz McColgan first.

What no one knew was that Tulu had a secret weapon. Japanese trainers had been assisting the Ethiopians since the team had not been accompanied by trainers. Tulu was also receiving expert Japanese acupuncture treatment.

On the day before the final the Chuo University lecturer Yasutada Sato gave Tulu a massage and inserted small acupuncture needles at several points on her body. Sato told her to keep them in until race-day morning. The only physical weakness Sato found in her Ethiopian athlete was in the right ankle. 'I advise her to tape her ankle when she races.' Supplying two rolls of tape, Sato sent Tulu off saying, 'Promise me you will win.'

No one knows if Tulu promised.

Britain had been having an abysmal championship so far. No gold medals, too few of the rest. Roger Black, known to his fan club as 'sex on legs', had won only silver although, as he kept saying, 'I should have won, it was my race.' Linford Christie, whose personal best of 9.92 seconds in the hundred metres had placed him only fourth, was talking about retiring. And the former world champion, golden boy Steve Cram, the world record holder at the mile, was watching the championships in a Tokyo hotel room, injured.

'It's hard on those who have not run,' Liz said. 'This is an individual sport but when people don't win medals, it's definitely depressing for the team as a whole.'

On Friday, 30 August, a stifling evening in Tokyo, the South African Elana Meyer was one of the sixty thousand people seated in the stadium. Dark-haired Meyer, who had displaced Zola Budd as an Afrikaner heroine, had come to Tokyo primarily to watch Liz race. If South Africa were readmitted to international competition in time for next year's Olympics, petite Meyer would oppose Liz on the Barcelona track.

Just before the start of Liz's final, a couple of the British athletics correspondents on their way to the press box came upon Peter near the track, limbering up as though he were the one who was racing. They invited him to the press box, where he was sitting now waiting for the race to begin.

As Liz looked up at the stadium monitor that showed her and the other runners larger than life, there was already a furrow of sweat on her brow. Kristiansen would really need her white gloves tonight. The temperature and the humidity were pushing ninety. Tokyo felt like a steam bath.

At the gun, Liz ran to the front of the pack and kept going, the pack following, none of them eager to lead. Steve Cram, sitting in the BBC's hotel room watching the race, shook his head. It looked like she was going to do it the hard way, all twenty-five laps from the front. To a middle-distance runner like himself the 10,000 was always a gruelling race, but in that heat it would be a nightmare. And Liz was setting a murderous pace.

Could anyone possibly keep it up?

Behind her were Kathrin Ullrich, the Berliner now arriving at her prime, and Kristiansen, the defending champion, past it, but keeping up. There was also last year's world junior champion, the little Ethiopian Tulu. Behind them was a bedraggled file of runners in various stages of destruction.

The 74-second-per-lap pace was meant to be killing, its object was to grind them down. Liz herself felt it hurting, but she kept saying to herself, 'If you want this one you've got to work.' She just kept saying it. I want it, I want it. She wanted it so badly. What did it matter if it hurt?

If 74 or 75 seconds was too slow, if she wasn't going fast enough, if they were still with her at the end, then Ullrich or one of the others would kick past and leave her for dead. I want, Liz told herself, pushing forward, I want, I want. Ullrich fell back exhausted by the pace in this heat, her head beginning to loll. Liz kept going. Kristiansen vanished to seventh. Good. But with eight laps remaining Tulu, who had a devastating kick, was still on Liz's shoulder. Was it going to be another Seoul?

Liz could almost hear Peter telling her to pick it up, go faster. It was hard in that heat. With six and a half laps remaining, Tulu passed her. There was a momentary dread but within twenty-five metres Liz passed Tulu to avoid stepping on her feet. Tulu had gone to the front merely to slow the race down. When Liz passed, she could see Tulu was beaten. She had nothing left. There were still six laps to go. And it was sweltering.

Steve Cram frowned at the television screen. With no one pursuing Liz, with only her will as the engine, in this heat could she hang on?

'Win or lose,' Brendan Foster said to the television audience, 'this is the bravest run I've ever seen by a British runner.'

Peter in the press box was inscrutable.

I want, Liz chanted silently, and ran. Five more laps and it would be over, four more, three. It hurt. She was exhausted. It hurt. Two more. The two Chinese fighting each other for silver and bronze twenty seconds back were out of striking distance. The race was hers if she could last. I want it, she told herself as she pushed herself forward, I want, I want, I want, and she ran faster and faster. And then it was over. She was the world champion.

In the press box the athletics correspondents grin at Peter. He grins back. The happiness in the press box is palpable. But Peter has already warned them that he will have to hurry away at the end of the race, and 'spontaneously' run on to the track and embrace Liz, holding her Asics shoes. She signed with them shortly before the championships and wants to make sure that the new sponsor's shoes are seen at the victory. Now Peter rushes off to the track.

It goes as planned but is superseded by the huge emotion of the moment. He hugs her. They kiss. The cameras see. The whole nation rejoices.

Elated but exhausted, dripping from sweat, Liz does three-quarters of her lap of honour and when she arrives at the tunnel, the athletes' route out of the stadium, she ducks into it. Waiting for her are the British media who are ecstatic. They are, after all, British and there is nothing like a winner to get you a big by-line. Soon she's giggling and swigging water and hopping from foot to foot with excitement just as she did as a thirteen-year-old. 'I told you,' she reminds the scoffers of the media, 'I told you I'd do it. My head's screwed on. We did it. Me and Peter.'

On television, Brendan Foster has pronounced it 'the greatest performance by a male or female British athlete in the history of long-distance running'.

Ingrid Kristiansen's reaction is sourer: 'Liz is good, but she was a minute outside my world record.'

The Afrikaner who had come to size up the future opposition was not admitting it if she was intimidated. 'McColgan runs well, but she doesn't impress me that much. I could have done just as well.' And she would in Barcelona, Elana Meyer vowed, if South Africa were readmitted to international competition in time for the Olympics.

But no matter what anyone thought or pretended to think, this year would belong to Liz McColgan. 'This means the world to me because I've worked all my life to become a world champion.'

No other British woman had won a world-class title on the track except Ann Packer, whose Olympic gold medal twenty-seven years before, also in Tokyo, had been won the year Liz was born. There was to be no other British gold at the 1991 World Championships. Hard as it was to believe, things would get even better. It was going to be a magical year.

In November Liz made her debut in a world-class marathon, the New York. You might as well start at the top. She won it. Her time of two hours 27.32 seconds was the world's fastest first-time marathon by a woman.

The streets of New York were paved with gold, £25,000 in prize money and a Mercedes worth £20,000 plus a secret bonus and appearance money. She was even invited to the New York Stock Exchange to open trading by ringing the bell. Ronald Reagan was the only other outsider to have received this honour. Sports agents speculated that Liz could make half a million dollars a season.

It was a conservative figure.

Liz had returned to her old agent Kim McDonald who had offices in New York as well as London. Her picture would soon be appearing on the plastic wrappers of Mother's Pride bread. There were all sorts of deals. A firm of Scottish accountants was giving her £12,000 for two years. Grampian Television, another new sponsor, was paying £25,000, says her father. She would co-operate in two documentaries they wanted to make about her. There was much more.

Besides these great financial strides, Liz had in mind a leap forward in the marathon. In the next year or the next she hoped to break through the big psychological barrier, the 2:20. No woman had ever run a marathon in less than two hours twenty minutes. Liz wanted to be the first. Previously, only two women had even been thought capable of doing it, but neither had. One was Ingrid Kristiansen whose day was done, and the other was Joan Benoit-Samuelson who had won the first ever Olympic marathon in Los Angeles in 1984. Benoit-Samuelson once held the fastest time in the marathon. Soon after Mama Ingrid Kristiansen bettered her time, Benoit-Samuelson became pregnant. Her daughter Abigail was born in October of 1988, but neither she nor Kristiansen were ever able to break through the marathon barrier. Now the woman most mooted to do so was Eilish's mum.

There had been no victory parade in Dundee for Liz after Tokyo. The council was angry with her. On 'Wogan' Liz admitted she was miffed, but on the whole this was a winter of very great content, bringing triumphs, riches and honours, one great achievement tumbling over the next.

The British public voted Liz the BBC Sports Personality of the Year, ahead of all the men. Few women before her had had the honour. It was wonderful to join the sporting ranks of Virginia Wade, Fatima Whitbread and Princess Anne, the latter of whom she had already met on more than one occasion.

Liz had also nearly two years ago made the acquaintance of the Queen. At a dinner for the athletes in Auckland, in early 1990, Liz was sitting a few seats down the long table when the Queen whispered something to a retainer and Liz was asked to change with someone to a place nearer. Then Betty and Martin Lynch's youngest daughter Elizabeth, the skinny girl from the worst council estate in Dundee, found herself eating and drinking and chatting with Elizabeth Regina. The Queen, who knew a lot about sport and told Liz she liked to go swimming, easily drew the former Whitfield girl out.

To cap her miraculous year, her *annus mirabilis*, Liz was surprised to find herself the subject of *This Is Your Life*.

On the race track her stock went up and up. Liz had proved herself in the marathon and continued to show her great worth on the track. Kristiansen was out of it now. The queen was dead, long live the queen. Liz was demanding and getting big, big money for even the most ordinary international invitational races. And she was getting new respect even from officialdom and certainly from her rivals. In just one year she had attained almost everything a woman could wish for – fame, fortune and great personal happiness.

The grass looked greener on either side of the fence than you could reasonably have expected in winter light. The December sun was actually shining. Few people could expect to be paid £10,000 to run three miles in the country in fine weather, but the world champion certainly could. She was running the 5000-metre County Durham International Cross-country Race in rustic Beamish for the money. Why not?

As usual, the promoters wanted some titillating pre-race comments from their star and for once Liz played the role admirably. 'I honestly think this is the best ever cross-country race outside the world championships,' Liz said before it.

It was a huge exaggeration, but the promoters and the press were pleased with the quote.

The field was quite good. Two of Liz's fading old rivals were in the running: the once brilliant and once highly consistent twenty-six-year-old Kenyan Susan Sirma, and sturdy Olga Bondarenko, the Russian who had outkicked Liz for the gold medal in the bad old days of the 1988 Seoul Olympics. The memory could still make Liz wince. Although already thirty-two, Bondarenko would probably be there next year at the Barcelona Olympics. Fingers crossed.

That other fleet-footed Russian Yelena Romanova was in Beamish today too, as was the British up-and-comer Andrea Wallace.

The sun continued to shine as the runners did four laps up and down the hills of the grassy course, past the North of England open-air museum with its reconstructions of turn-of-the-century farm and village life. There was even a sort of colliery, one of the few working coal mines in the county. Each time Liz whizzed past the village bandstand they played her a signature tune.

Liz finished way ahead of Susan Sirma. Olga Bondarenko, worn out perhaps from too much standing in the Volgograd food queues, straggled in third, looking shattered.

After the race, Liz said: 'It felt like a training run. I've had harder sessions on my treadmill at home.'

Early in the new year, Liz set a world half marathon best in Japan and a world indoor 5000 metres record in Birmingham.

So, would she have another go at the World Cross-country Championship in March? This time it was in Boston. At the last minute, Liz decided, yes. In 1991, four months after Eilish's birth, Liz had been third in the race. This March, when the record books showed that she was virtually invincible, the whole world was expecting her to win.

The British team, apart from Liz and Peter who were training in Florida, flew to Boston on the same plane and they stayed at the same hotel. Liz and Peter stayed at another. Understandably Liz didn't crave the distraction of being in the midst of everyone, especially the press. But being in proximity to the team star would be the highlight of the trip for many of the team's newcomers.

No one sees much of Liz. A lone Peter represents the family at the pre-race banquet. Liz is at the hotel with Eilish.

Someone suggests to Liz's manager Kim McDonald that it might be diplomatic to have Liz meet the team. Won't it be embarrassing, McDonald is asked, if some of the youngsters are asked by their friends and their families what Liz is like when they return home and they can only say they never met her?

As Britain's previous world champions have accepted, a star has certain responsibilities. Inspiring the youngsters is one of them. McDonald promises to whisper a word in Liz's ear. There's plenty of time. The race is not till Saturday.

It was muddy when the runners walked the course on the Wednesday. On Thursday the snows came, heavy and deep. Veterans' races on Friday chopped up the course so much that the Bostonians decided to have the surface flattened. Then the weather turned colder.

Walking the course again on Friday, which the new snow has made necessary, the runners noticed that it gets treacherous where the machines have packed down the snow. 'It was more like sheet ice in some places,' recalls eighteen-year-old Paula Radcliffe, who would be running in the junior event.

To Radcliffe, Liz hadn't looked herself as she walked the course. Not ill exactly, but tired around the eyes which were slightly red, as though she were fighting something off. This one was a proper cross-country course, with hills, trees and snow-covered open fields. Not as elsewhere in some years when the World Cross-country Championships course had been quite flat, laid on for the TV cameras.

On the Saturday the World Junior Championship preceded the main event. Paula Radcliffe, whose prospects were not tremendous – she was racing in large part to get experience – had trouble choosing her spikes. 'I thought about it a lot, I changed them about three times. I ended up with fifteen-millimetre spikes in the front two, and twelve in all the others.'

Liz felt ill, but since she hadn't been at the team banquet – she hadn't been in evidence at all – she went down to the start where the juniors were finishing off their warm-ups and getting ready to go into the start pens.

'Good luck, Paula,' Liz called.

Radcliffe was delighted. 'She just came down and wished us all good luck, and she spoke to me a bit.'

A month before, when Liz had broken the world indoor 5000-metre record, Radcliffe had been in the race. Still growing in athletics terms, she'd finished fairly far behind Liz. After that race, Liz went as usual to see the team physio. She was still in the physio room when she saw Paula Radcliffe returning from routine drug testing.

'How did you get on?' Liz asked. She meant the race; the drug test was no problem.

Radcliffe mumbled her finishing time.

'That's inside the British junior record,' Liz said.

Radcliffe hadn't realized.

'You definitely broke the old record.'

Liz's interest meant a lot to Radcliffe. 'I think of her as someone famous and far away. I don't actually know Liz to talk to. Just the occasional word.'

In the junior race, Radcliffe's race, she soon realized that her choice of spikes had been exactly right. 'But a lot of people were slipping. In my race some of the young Kenyans didn't have any spikes on or anything, they were just running on bare feet. I didn't slip at all.'

She also went very fast, and to the astonishment of many she won. There was elation. No one had expected a British world *junior* cross-country champion.

Now it was time for the senior race. No points there for guessing the favourite. But for the first time in a long while, Liz wasn't looking forward to racing. The proper Bostonians had chosen a proper cross-country course. It would be a difficult but an interesting race.

An improper course might have been preferable the way she was feeling today. But she was there on the start line, and it was time to go. Ignoring her disinclination, bare-legged but in gloves and a long-sleeved shirt, Liz ran, rounding a field first of all, then up the hill through that wooded bit, fast if possible. It wasn't possible.

Liz found herself slipping occasionally as she ran, but that was by no means the worst of it. The worst was that her legs were stuck in first gear. They would scarcely move. Other runners were passing her.

If she could get to the top of this horrible hill – rather, when she got to the top of it – there would be momentum on the way down. That might get her into second gear. It did, but the other runners were passing her as though she was standing still.

She kept on, unable to shift even into third gear, knowing that what was needed in a championship race was fourth or fifth. Her race was a nonstarter but she kept on. Down the hill and back into the fields she went and on for another loop of the same.

Her throat hurt, there was a purplish coldsore on her lower lip and no energy in her legs, but Liz ploughed on because it was her nature to complete whatever she started, and for the sake of the team, which would get points if she finished. Arriving at the stadium at last, she crossed the line an ignominious forty-first. It was the first time in her career that it would be major news that Liz had met defeat.

As if a bad cold and a bad race were not trouble enough, some of the media reported that Liz had haughtily refused Paula Radcliffe's pre-race offer of the tried and tested spikes.

'Oh, no. I didn't offer them. That sort of got blown up by the press,' Radcliffe explains. 'All that happened was that one of the team managers came round asking if anyone had any spare spikes. I said I had a spare set of spikes the same as I'd worn. So I gave them to him, and I think he offered them to Liz but she decided not to use them. I think she only had six millimetres in.'

Radcliffe lives just outside Bedford, which is not known for its cold weather. Had she run in snow before? 'Not very often, but when it does snow I do still train in it.'

Radcliffe's victory, despite her inexperience of the weather and the world-class competition, would be used by some of the press as another stick with which to beat Liz. There was plenty of snow in Scotland. But these days Liz hid from the snow, training indoors on her electric treadmill. She had bought it partly because Kristiansen had one – and look what happened to Kristiansen! Had Liz become too used to the comforts of home, too soft?

What had become of the Whitfield girl who used to run for miles through the snow in wellies?

In his dismay at the defeat, Peter reveals he is having the same problem with his athlete other coaches have had. Liz wouldn't ease off her training before this race. Clearly she is ill. But she is also tired. Maybe now she would listen to him when he told her not to run all those miles, he says to several people in Boston. They print it in their newspapers.

They leave the New England snow for Florida, where Liz and Peter have a condominium. There are trails and natural paths to run on in Gainsville, and access to the University of Florida's track. With her eye on the Barcelona Olympics, Liz plans to train and road race in America till the last days of May, and then start her season on the track in Britain. The original plan had been to be based in Gainsville from January to May.

There has already been one unplanned transatlantic journey because Eilish had eczema and Liz wanted her to see their regular doctor. Now, in mid-April, even though Liz's sister Karen and her husband and children are over for a visit, the stay is again cut short.

For one thing, there are the grisly unsolved Gainsville murders of teenaged girls. For another, Martin Lynch, left on his own – Betty is here helping out with Eilish – was found by his son on the floor. He had blacked out. Liz is worried about her father. Another factor may be that there are too many visitors in Gainsville or that Liz misses home. They fly to Scotland.

Tests at Ninewells Hospital show that Martin is all right. 'I was no eating properly,' he says.

'Men never eat properly on their own,' says Vi Bennett, who has heard about his blackout. 'Thank goodness he now seems fine.'

'I can't get any stronger, but I can get faster,' Liz had announced in the spring. With speed in mind, on Tuesday and Thursday evenings, Liz and Peter have a night out with the boys on the tartan track at Dundee's Caird Park. Their training partners, members of the Hawkhill Harriers, are all male because none of their club's female runners could possibly keep up. Liz and Peter have been training with the Hawkhill lads for years.

'We train harder and longer when Liz is here,' Cookie, one of the regulars, says. 'If Liz is away racing or something, we may start training fifteen minutes late, chatting and that.' No nonsense. 'If she is here, there is no chat, we start dead on time. And run two seconds faster.'

In early May it is necessary to re-cross the Atlantic for the three lucrative races in the States Liz is under contract to run. The 8K race in Washington, DC, offers $75,000 (nearly £40,000) and something more than money, a chance to avenge herself against the World Cross-country Champion Lynn Jennings. In Washington, now virus free, Liz gives her all and the winning shoe is on the other foot.

In Central Park, running in the New York mini-marathon, Liz and the other runners are furious at having to dodge roller-skaters and strolling toddlers. For reasons known only to themselves, officials hadn't roped off the route. A collision could have caused someone serious harm, and in avoiding one Liz could easily have torn a muscle or ligament.

But there is no mishap. Liz wins this, the third of her races – the first one has been in Ohio. Her takings for the three weeks in May top $100,000. Now home to Scotland, en route to Barcelona.

— 14 —

No Pain, No Spain

The car pulled into the drive of Woodfield House past the row of infant evergreens Liz's father had planted. In the short time she and Peter had been away in America summer had come to Arbroath. There was no hint of the icy May gales that had been blowing across the track on the night of their last training session at Caird Park.

Good. It was time for the final stage of her Olympic build-up. It would be helpful to have the Scottish weather as an ally.

The plan was to do some short, sharp races. The prime purpose was to make sure that Barcelona was a replay of Tokyo and not of Seoul. At Tokyo Liz had been fast enough and had exuded sufficient single-minded and unswerving determination to break the spirit of the opposition by front-running the whole race. She and Peter had thoroughly discussed her race tactics, but in the heat of the moment Liz ignored them.

'We never thought I would lead from start to finish. We never even discussed it,' she says. 'There was a lot of good people in the race and I didn't want to get boxed. I said "I'm going to run a good first lap anyway to keep out of trouble." I felt really good and I kept going.'

'I was totally amazed,' Peter says, 'when I saw her there, and I just thought she must be feeling really good.'

It had been a very brave race.

Her Afrikaner rival Elana Meyer had not been the only rival watching it. In the year that followed every 10,000-metre runner of stature was gazing intently at her video of Liz's World Championship race, frame by frame, and plotting how to beat her.

This was the nature of the world of sport. At judo champion-ships, for example, one of the jobs of team managers is zooming in with camcorders on the opposition's bouts.

With Seoul as an object lesson, Tokyo an inspiration and Bar-celona in mind, the focus of Liz's training and her racing prior to the Games would be on her finishing speed. She had upped her pace over the last 2000 metres in Tokyo. Now she had to be sure she could do it again, faster.

Years of long runs had given Liz endurance aplenty, but she was still largely a one-pace runner, able to up the pace a bit but lacking the devastating kick of an Yvonne Murray or a Bonda-renko or an Elana Meyer at the end of a race. Was it too late to develop a finishing kick like Bondarenko's, like Sebastian Coe's?

Olga Bondarenko had not been born with the ability to finish with a flourish. In kick-building sessions once a fortnight during the Russian winter and once a week as the summer competition season drew near, she had been taught to run very fast when her fatigue was greatest. How? Bondarenko would run 400 metres fast on the Volgograd track and recover by jogging another 400. Then she'd do 300 metres faster, recovering over 300. Then 200 faster still, and so on. Running faster despite these decreasing recovery intervals she got used to going quicker the more tired she felt.

You could also work on speed by doing fast set repetitions, say, six times 300 metres, honing your speed by running a series of short, sharp races in which speed would have to be more important than endurance. This latter was the principle that Liz decided to rely on along with sessions on the track. She would never have a devastating kick but she could bring up her overall race pace and leave enough in reserve to go a little faster on the laps.

In the 1500 and 3000 races she would run this season the oppo-sition would be good runners who were specialists in those dis-tances. Running under-distance meant Liz would risk losing races in the build-up to the Olympics, and that, of course, might have other dangerous consequences. But it was a risk, she and Peter decided, that was worth taking.

*

Within a week of her Scottish homecoming, Liz was to run her first race. There had been the usual fuss when Liz informed officials that she had absolutely no intention of running at her Olympic distance before the Games. They threatened to drop her from the Olympic team unless she ran it either in the UK Championships or the Olympic Trials. Liz stuck to her guns. A tiring twenty-five-lap 10,000-metre race so close to the Games would harm rather than help her preparation.

Officialdom spluttered, but eventually, as Liz knew they would for their foremost female star, they caved in and she and Peter went south to Sheffield for the UK Championships at the Don Valley Stadium.

The place had memories. It was to race here last winter that Liz had argued the Big Bad Wolf of British athletics up to £10,000 in appearance money. He'd offered her much less. 'But I'm the world champion,' her father heard her fairly shout into the telephone to the promoter Andy Norman, the most powerful man in the sport.

As Norman well knew, she was Britain's *only* world champion and therefore very bankable, and so, although the top male stars including Linford Christie and Roger Black were getting only £7000, he says, Liz got her £10,000.

From a runner's point of view, Don Valley, the only new stadium built in Britain in the last thirty years, at a price tag of £30 million, is awkwardly sited. The crosswind that comes off the hills behind the city smacks runners in the face and makes setting a world record much less likely than chill or injury. Even though it was nearly June, on this Saturday night the runners were doing their warm-ups indoors.

As usual immediately before a competition, Liz hardly talked to anyone except Peter. This race was her domestic debut of the season, and she seemed nervous. Even though the field was not top class, she was running way under-distance in the 1500 metres, and risked defeat. Peter was entered in the steeplechase, which he hoped to run in Barcelona. Liz did a few silent stretches.

Around her the Don Valley's huge indoor warm-up area was a hubbub of activity. Runners were jogging on the industrial grey carpet, keeping carefully within the painted white lanes. Linford

Christie, who liked to talk to anyone except the press, stood joking with John Regis who was being rubbed down by a masseur right in the middle of everything.

Fatima Whitbread came over and said hello. Kirsty Wade stopped briefly to chat. Liz and Kirsty were not in the same 1500 metres heat tonight, but tomorrow they would race each other in the final. There were so many similarities between them. Kirsty, too, had made a comeback after having a baby, but with less childcare than Liz had and a health club to run, Kirsty had not done as well on the track. Her husband was closely involved in her training, too, although periodically Kirsty still saw Harry Wilson who for years had been her coach.

Now Liz did a few more stretches. Then she lay down on one of the wooden benches, her back flat, her knees bent, retreating to somewhere inside herself.

When Liz and the other runners in her 1500 metres heat lined up on the track, it was early evening but the sun glowed, like the vest Liz wore to run in, a bright yellow. Like most experienced racers, Liz knew that there was no need to blow the field away in her heat. As long as she finished in the top three she was assured of a place in the final. Conserving her energy, Liz calmly finished third.

Meanwhile there was a storm brewing in the press box. Instead of wearing her blue and white Dundee Hawkhill Harriers club vest, as the rules required for the UK Championships, Liz had raced in the golden vest which had her sponsor's name writ large on it. No one was allowed to advertise a sponsor at these particular championships. Would she do it again tomorrow in the final, which would be televised?

The media requested that Liz come up to be interviewed in the press box. It is standard procedure for athletes to go to the press box after a race to answer questions, though it is not obligatory. Steve Cram, John Regis and Eamon Martin had been up there already this weekend. Liz refused.

As an athlete, it was her right. In most other sports it would not have been. Graf, Seles, Navratilova and other tennis players have no choice but to appear at the post-match press conference if asked for by any member of the media.

After warming down, Liz went out to watch Peter run his steeplechase heat. She sat in the front row of the stands, nonchalantly pulling on two extra layers of clothing as she waited for the start, ending up with a layer of violently violet bottoms beneath a white hooded sweatshirt top. Peter, running in Hawkhill colours, finished fourth. He wouldn't make the final. His running had been suffering as he concentrated on hers.

Two male journalists spotted Liz in the stands. But they didn't go to her, as was their right, to ask her any questions about the vest infringement.

Why not?

'Because they don't like a woman to tell them to go away,' the formidable Andy Norman said wryly on Sunday morning. Instructions had been given and it would be made perfectly plain to Liz, albeit politely, he said, that she could not race except in club colours. Quite apart from it being against the rules, it was unfair to the many other athletes who had endorsement contracts.

Indeed, Fatima Whitbread, retired from the javelin and now administrator of the elite, sponsor-rich Chafford Hundred, wondered, 'If Liz can get away with promoting her sponsors at this meeting, why can't we?'

Norman is engaged to Fatima.

Secondly, if Liz got away with it, it would be a foot in the door for further commercialization of the UK Championships. To defenders of the old ways, many of them journalists, this was the route to Sodom and Gomorrah.

'But couldn't it be,' I asked, 'that Liz simply hadn't had a clean club vest to wear?'

Everyone roared with laughter at my naivete. 'As you Americans would say,' one of the insiders quipped, 'the issue is money, honey.'

Although no one mentioned it at the time, I discovered later that Liz had had vest trouble before. ITV had threatened to pull the plug on her the first time, in 1986, when she wore Reebok clothing with the symbol large and visible instead of her club vest. At the time Norman had said: 'We accept Liz made an innocent mistake, but we will be contacting the company to ensure that such mistakes don't happen again.'

Now it *was* happening again. For sure, money is a motivating fact, but I also wondered if the issue wasn't as much about independence. Liz had, since girlhood, always wanted to do what she wanted to do.

At noon the team manager, Joan Allison, whom no one had bothered to tell about the problem, hurried from the Swallow Hotel where the team was staying to the track to try to smoothe things over. Informing Liz about vest etiquette wasn't Joan's job. Someone else should have done that. But smoothing things over was. However, when Joan got to Liz a couple of hours before the final, she was not entirely surprised to hear from Liz that no one else had even mentioned the vest to her.

As he drove to the track for the afternoon's finals, Andy Norman took a call on the car phone. TV was lopping six minutes off the time they would devote to the UK Championships. The TV people had some sort of schedule conflict. Andy sighed. Roger Black's 400-metre race, scheduled for 3.08 p.m. simply would not be televised unless Andy did some fancy organizational footwork.

You couldn't tell unless you looked at the clock, but Andy saw to it that the intervals between the races were whittled down. Half a minute here, a minute there. The prize-giving ceremonies ever so slightly brisker.

That is why events were running a few minutes ahead of schedule when Liz stepped on to the track at 2.34 p.m. for the 1500 metres final. Instead of the blue and white of Dundee Hawkhill Harriers, Liz had on her sponsor's vest. Asics did them in several colours, and this one was a brazen red.

The starter's pistol fired. Liz soon took the lead and looked poised to win until suddenly the pack, all of them 1500-metre specialists, swarmed past. Liz crossed the line fifth.

Fatima, watching the race in a VIP seat in the stands, said, 'The public don't understand that it doesn't matter at all if Liz wins or loses at fifteen hundred metres, since it is not her event. She was just running it to get in some speed practice.' It had been brave of Liz to take on the specialists at their own game.

Steve Ovett, in the commentary box, said, 'In that company, Liz will be pleased with that.'

She wasn't.

'I ran only one decent lap in the race,' Liz chided herself.

And to underline that she could do much better, she returned to the track two hours later to run the 3000 metres in which she hadn't even been entered. And won it.

Channel 4, which had long since signed off from the championships, missed the story, and although Sky probably caught it Liz had run the race almost solely to prove something to herself. Ullrich and the Kenyan Susan Sirma, who were racing each other at 3000 metres in the Rome Grand Prix on Tuesday, would also get the message.

In a race that had been an afterthought, Liz picked up another crown. She was now the United Kingdom 3000-metre champion. That would show them that she was not a one-pace runner, wouldn't it?

Life is not so simple. There were grumbles because the rules had been bent to let her enter. Entries had closed two weeks ago on 23 May, and at least one other runner who wanted to enter after that date had been refused.

But the person who should have been most upset, Lisa York who came second in the race, took Liz's late entry in her stride. 'If I had won it, I would always know it was because Liz wasn't running,' the up-and-coming twenty-two-year-old UK cross-country champion said philosophically. 'All that really mattered to me was that I ran a good race.' Lisa York had done the double, too, finishing third in the earlier 1500-metre race, but she had been entered in both races on time.

At last, Liz gave an audience to the journalists.

'Are you frightened of Elana Meyer, Liz?' one of them predictably asked.

'Not really.'

The South African gazelle Elana Meyer was an unknown quantity. She was definitely fast. Indeed, her times set in South Africa were phenomenal. But because South Africa had previously been barred from international competition, Elana Meyer had never run among the best, and who knew how she would stand up to the pace amid the rough and tumble of pumping elbows and painful spikes?

'People are getting caught up in Elana Meyer versus Liz McColgan,' Liz said. 'There are runners training hard all over the world. When I go to the line there are thirty other girls who could beat me.'

But she didn't think any of them would.

Her nine-year-old at school and the baby asleep, Christine Haskett Price finds a moment to leaf through the new issue of *Athletics Today*, the runners' equivalent of the *Radio Times*. At forty Harry's first star is still a useful runner in her age group. Turning to an article written by Cliff Temple, who is her former coach as well as athletics' *Sunday Times* man, she reads Liz's explanation of why she wasn't wearing a Dundee Hawkhill Club vest. This is a big issue to club runners.

'Officials did make a point of speaking to me about it,' Liz allows, 'but they accepted that I do not run for a club. People always say Dundee Hawkhill but I have not run for them for seven years, although I am actually an honorary life member.'

Christine Price moved to Bolton years ago and hasn't been a member of Dundee Hawkhill for a long time. But as she reads Liz's answer, she is taken aback.

What must the regulars at Dundee Hawkhill, the lads who make themselves available on Tuesday and Thursday evenings to train with Liz, or the kids who held up the batons at Liz and Peter's wedding, feel when they read or hear about what Liz has said?

Christine reads on. The author, Cliff Temple, muses: 'And if she has not been a member of a British club for seven years, and therefore paid no subscriptions, then is she even eligible for the UK Championships? Or if the honorary membership of Dundee theoretically precludes the need to pay subs, then should she not have been required by officials to at least borrow Peter's vest?'

The McColgan–Murray rivalry has been compared to that of Seb Coe and Steve Ovett. Yvonne Murray beat Liz when they were

girls running in the Scottish Schools Cross-country Championships, and frequently after, until Liz moved up to her proper
distance. Both were medallists at the Seoul Olympics, dominance
see-sawing when Yvonne Murray became the European 3000-
metre champion, until Liz decisively became Number One when
she won the world championship. Theirs is an old rivalry, complicated, deep.

On the one hand, the rivalry between the two women is more
intense than Coe and Ovett's because there is only one spot for
a British golden girl, and there were potentially two. Three, four,
half a dozen top perches exist for male runners. But there is less
room on the sports pages and the sports programmes for women.

On the other hand, the rivalry is less intense than Coe–Ovett's
for two reasons: firstly because Liz and Yvonne's events are different, and secondly because Yvonne's interpretation of femininity requires her to smoothe things over.

Unlike Coe and Ovett, Liz and Yvonne welcome the prospect
of running against each other. A year ago there had been hell to
pay when Yvonne won in a very close race at Edinburgh's famous
Meadowbank Stadium, and Liz complained bitterly of being
spiked or nearly spiked.

Tonight there was to be a rematch between the two women at
Meadowbank, and the headlines in Scotland were predicting
blood on the track. Keeping to her training plan Liz was running
the 3000 metres, Murray's distance.

From the grassy warm-up area behind the stadium you can see
the city's grey stone houses. Neither Liz nor Yvonne seemed to
notice the scenery or each other as they warmed up. Each ran
past the other as though she wasn't there. This could be put down
entirely to concentration, except that Liz said a word here and
there to other people. So did Yvonne.

At the starter's gun, Liz raced forward fast, and there they
were again, Liz frowning with effort, Yvonne running at her
heels. Then Liz ran faster, faster, faster, Yvonne straining at her
heels, Yvonne's cheeks redder with exertion than Liz's. They ran
neck and neck, Yvonne hovering at Liz's shoulder as they sped,
and just as the commentator began to think Liz might hold
Yvonne off this time, with 150 metres to go she surged past. It

was the quickest 3000 run in Europe of the season and the golden girls of Scotland had given the home crowd a fine race. They cheered.

In front of the cameras, in front of the crowd, in front of everyone, Yvonne embraced Liz warmly. Liz stood stock still for a split-second, seemingly wary, and then she returned the embrace. Yvonne had wanted badly to end those interminable stories of enmity, and she had done it with a single symbolic gesture.

The crowd signalled its approval.

Liz grins. 'I make a good pace-maker, don't I?'

'You think so, do you?'

'Aye.'

Yvonne smiles at Liz's good humour.

Now to the prize-giving in the centre of the stadium, Yvonne hurriedly pulling on her black track-suit bottoms over her shorts, Liz just in her shorts.

Liz has reason to feel exhilarated. Her time was quick, demonstrating to anyone who understands enough that she does have more than just one pace and she can speed up towards the end of a race. Liz and Yvonne are in high spirits, joking. It was a great run.

It was Yvonne's preferred distance at Meadowbank, so of course Yvonne won. Liz was brave as hell to run it. Not just to face losing, but to face the incomprehension that so many spectators would feel. But Liz cares much, much less than most of us what people think. That's her nature.

After the prize-giving, Liz hurries to the warm-up area to put some clothes on before her muscles go stiff. As she burrows for another layer of clothing in her well-used black canvas bag, Yvonne calls out:

'Hey, Liz, look what you did to me.' Her tone is good-natured. They are well away from everyone. Liz stops what she is doing and walks over. Yvonne plops down on to the grass, pulls down the front of her black track suit trousers and points at her leg.

Liz kneels on the grass to look.

There are spike marks on the front of Yvonne's right leg. One of the reasons Yvonne covered up so quickly after the race was to prevent anyone noticing them.

'I'm sorry,' Liz says.

Yvonne waves the incident away. 'It was an accident,' she says.

They decide to warm down together on the little track way behind the stadium. Liz hasn't really talked to Yvonne for a long time. Liz has been busy toing and froing across the Atlantic and Yvonne has just come back from fourteen weeks in South Africa, training at altitude. It was that South African sojourn, Liz can only imagine, that turbo-charged Yvonne enough to put in the fastest 3000 metres in Europe of the year so early in the season. That and Liz's racing her.

Liz knows Yvonne likes South Africa. Even before she went to South Africa, Yvonne was partial to South Africans. The reason is Zola Budd, now Zola Pieterse. While most people remember Zola for jumping the UK passport queue or colliding with Mary Decker Slaney at the LA Olympics, Yvonne's memory is quite different.

'When Zola came over a lot of the British women went negative about it. To me this was great having someone of that calibre to run against. The few times I went with her I blew up disastrously but every time I just kept chipping away, chipping away, and I got closer and closer to her.

'I used her as a standard of excellence to aim for. One day, someone asked me, "Do you think you could beat her?" And I realized the answer was yes. At the two thousand at Crystal Palace, I ran out of my skin, and I remember the last hundred metres coming out on her shoulder thinking, should I be here? This isn't right. And then I sprinted past her and knew it was. It was an amazing feeling. I beat Zola twice that year, once at Crystal Palace, once when I finished ahead of her at the European Championships in Stuttgart.'

That was where Liz had hooked up with John Anderson.

'I have a lot of respect for Zola,' Yvonne says, sticking to a safe subject. 'People keep writing her off but you've got to respect her.'

People keep writing her off not just because she has got fatter

and therefore slower, but because the South Africans have a new
star, Elana Meyer.

'I met Elana and she is a lovely person,' Yvonne tells me. I
doubt she would put it quite that way to Liz.

In the press room they are waiting for Liz and Yvonne. Liz
knows there will be more questions about the McColgan–Murray
rivalry and about Elana Meyer. Why bother? She continues
warming down when Yvonne blithely goes off to face the journalists.

On her way to the press conference. Yvonne has two interviews
lined up, one of them with me.

'How was your dinner with Elana Meyer?' I begin.

'I didn't go. Elana's husband, who was quite amusing at the
time, phoned me up and said, "We'd like to invite you to dinner.
To be perfectly honest about it, we want to get the lowdown on
Liz McColgan."

'And I thought, well I'm very patriotic and I would never do
that to another fellow athlete. So I just kept my distance. I
declined the offer.'

'Where is Liz?' they ask the press officer discreetly when Yvonne
walks into the press room on her own.

'She's still warming down. She will be here later.'

'This race was different in feeling from last year's, wasn't it,
Yvonne?' someone begins. 'Before the race they were saying
there was going to be blood on the track.'

'There will always be rivalry between me and Liz, but we're
friends off the track. People don't seem to realize it. We warmed
down together.'

'Didn't you accidentally spike her last year?'

'There would have been an official complaint, and there
wasn't,' Yvonne says evenly. As Liz, thoroughly warmed down,
heads Dundeeward with Peter, Yvonne explains that all that
aggro about last year's race was a sordid mistake.

'Being typical women, after a race we have to let off steam.
Both myself and Liz wanted to win last year, but there can only
be one winner. She was letting off steam to a friend who unfortunately turned out to be a journalist. But the next time I saw her

– it was at the World Championships – Liz came up to me and apologized, she felt so bad about it. It had bothered her all that time.'

There were sceptical looks on assorted faces.

'No one knows exactly who is on drugs, but we are all cynics,' the editor of *Athletics Today*, Randall Northam, tells me. But he, Cliff Temple and most of the others are adamant that Liz is not on drugs. 'Why not?' 'Just a hunch,' says Randall.

'Too scientific for her,' says his young correspondent specializing in women's sport, Duncan Mackay. 'Liz is a natural runner.' Indeed, according to Anderson he couldn't persuade her to go for preventive medical screenings, which can diagnose anaemia, or nutritional deficiencies or viruses before they do any harm.

A steady build-up of fast times rather than a sudden burst is regarded as the sign of a clean athlete. An athlete coming from nowhere to win a big competition would be most suspect. Liz's history shows a sufficiently gradual improvement.

Without a doubt, though, if she ever chose to use it, EPO and blood-doping could help an endurance runner like Liz. So could the carefully administered anabolic steroids. EPO, or erythropoietin, stimulates the body's production of red blood cells which increases stamina. Anabolic steroids, essentially the male hormone testosterone, build muscle and aggression, making athletes stronger and allowing them to train harder. Sometimes athletes on steroids fly into rages known as 'roid rages.

Random drug testing of the athletes in Britain is more thorough than in many places, but there are few who believe it can't happen here. But Liz, our girl? To a man, the athletics correspondents say no.

Drugs were much on the mind because Katrin Krabbe, the German golden girl, and the two other German sprinters banned for four years following a drugs test five months ago were in London hoping for a reprieve. Gnawing at their fingernails as they listened uncomprehending to the decision of the IAAF tribunal, Krabbe, Grit Breur and Silke Moeller, none of whom understood English, had to wait an extra hour for a German translation. However unlikely, it was just possible, the tribunal concluded, that the urine samples had been tampered with by malevolent persons unknown on their way from South Africa to Germany.

The three women were reprieved. They could compete in Barcelona. Their change of fortune, though a telling reflection of Olympic morality, did not, of course, affect Liz McColgan's chances directly in any way. But Gwen Torrence of Georgia, who had come second to Krabbe in Tokyo in both the hundred and two hundred metres, had not been looking forward to seeing her in Barcelona.

On the same day Krabbe was reprieved, the South African woman who was likely to be Liz McColgan's greatest threat in Barcelona stepped on to the track for her very first race in Europe.

15

Blood on the Track

'Have you heard?' Tony Ward, the press officer and Linford Christie's biographer, saunters into the Birmingham Olympic Trials press room trying to hide the satisfaction he feels. 'Has everyone heard? Elana Meyer has been defeated.'

Stepping off the plane from South Africa and virtually on to the Dutch track, she had been beaten to the 3000-metre line by Sonia O'Sullivan, the chestnut-haired Irish 3000-metre specialist. The boys in the press box shrug. So what? Meyer had underestimated how much the travelling would tire her, and like Liz she had chosen to run under-distance.

Like Liz, who would be defeated in all but one of the short, under-distance races she was to run against world-class opposition before the Olympics, Meyer had taken a calculated risk.

Like Liz, who kept running gutsily harder than was necessary and losing in races that were heartbreaking to watch, Meyer was conserving energy and honing her speed for the race that mattered, their confrontation in the Olympic 10,000.

On the road to Barcelona, Elana Meyer would be running only one race long enough to presage her Olympic prospects. Her 5000, in Stockholm in five days, would be a race to watch.

Liz's eyes lock on to the television screen as her most dangerous rival lines up on the Stockholm track. The starter's pistol fires. The hired pace-maker breaks to the front, and the slight, five-foot-one-inch tall South African follows, leaving the rest of the field far behind. Her dark, cropped head held high, Elana runs and runs, her back elegantly straight. The pace-making is imperfect, and Liz knows what irate thoughts must be rushing through her rival's head because Elana needs to run a very fast time in this 5000-metre race to throw down the gauntlet and put a scare into you know who.

At three thousand metres, still hugely in front, Meyer is left to make her own pace, and it is soon evident that she is slowing. Fatigue? No, her head bobs, her eyes wander. A failure of concentration. Liz never fails to concentrate.

Even as Liz watches, the South African pulls herself together, her laps quicken and she crosses the line in the very quick time of 14 minutes 51.42 seconds, the fastest time run by a woman this year, though Meyer herself has twice run faster in the past year. It is faster by over nine seconds than Liz had ever run the distance. The gauntlet is lying on the Arbroath floor.

The ever-prurient media inquire: had she seen Meyer's race?

She hadn't watched it live, she says. Perhaps she couldn't bear to. The video was live enough.

'Well, Liz, what is your assessment of Meyer's performance?' An obvious question which gets an obvious answer.

'It was good.'

But her own performance in Oslo in two days' time, she believes, will be even better.

Meanwhile, in Germany, the saga of the three reinstated German sprinters was reaching an unexpected climax. Katrin Krabbe and company, turning up at their club track for a spot of training, were met by officials eager to administer to each of them a drugs test. The very next day the women announced they were pulling out of Barcelona. These tests proved positive.

And in South Africa, where their bogus urine specimens had been detected, two more athletes were banned for drug abuse. This time, both were South Africans.

In Oslo, where Liz McColgan will be running her only pre-Olympic race that matters, the media again play the Elana card. Tomorrow at the famous Bislett Games Liz is running the 5000, as Elana did. Half their Olympic distance. 'Will you be trying to go faster than Elana?'

. 'I'm just after a fast time. I hope I'll run a personal best.'

Five years ago in this Oslo stadium Liz ran her fastest ever 5000 metres, in a time of 15 minutes 1.08 seconds, beating Kristiansen and establishing herself as heiress apparent. But she had never been able to better Ingrid's long-standing 14 minute 37.33 second world record set here six years ago. No one had. If Liz could do it in the run-up to the Olympics, not only would there be this season's first glory but there would be gold.

A 'handsome' payment, so the papers said. But handsomeness is in the eyes of the beholder. One woman's handsome is another's brute. In fact, my sources told me, Liz's appearance money was less than usual, which at British meetings was now $20,000 (£10,000).

Here at Bislett, where the paymaster was Andy Norman's former brother-in-law and current business associate, Svene Arne Hanson, Liz was getting only $12,500 (roughly £6000) in appearance money, with a $25,000 bonus if she broke the world 5000-metre record.

To Liz McColgan, who had recently turned down $200,000 to run in the London Marathon, even with all her expenses paid, the Bislett appearance money was hardly hunky.

The pay cut was a classic case of market forces. Whereas the McVitie meeting had been built around Liz, they didn't really need her at Bislett as they had plenty of stars.

Actually, Liz McColgan needed them. She wanted the prestige of winning at Bislett, she needed the pre-Olympic competition and the stadium was known to be world-record prone.

Hence the scant $25,000 on offer for a world record. The only thing good to be said about it was that an identical amount was on offer for a men's world javelin record. Men nearly always got more, although Andy and Arne were remarkably good feminists and far more enlightened than most on the issue of equal pay.

Liz's alleged mercenariness, her insistence on high appearance money, get a lot of play in the press. 'The sports correspondents are jealous,' Norman said when the same thing happened to Fatima. 'It's not so bad if a talented male athlete makes more money than they do. But they can't stand it if it's a woman.'

At the next grand prix world champion Yobes Ondieki, the Kenyan who had quarrelled with John Anderson, stood to make a $50,000 bonus for breaking the men's world 5000-metre record. The Algerian world 1500 metres champion Hassiba Boulmerka, only a woman, was being offered a bonus of less than a third of that, $13,500, for a record in the mile. The difference wasn't the distance. It was gender.

A dozen years ago the American runner Mary Decker, not yet Slaney, broke a world record and was paid, she told me proudly – though not for publication then, as it was still illegal – an under-the-table bonus of $3000 (£2000). Although at the time Mary Decker was America's golden girl, at the height of both her fame and earning power, she could not command the same fee as the then pre-eminent Kenyan Henry Rono. He routinely got $6000. Double the money.

Fair is by no means fair in women's athletics; parity is largely unknown. With very few exceptions, equal opportunity is still regarded as a wild idea in sport. So if Liz didn't speak up for herself, if she didn't keep arguing for more money for herself, who would?

In her terms, Bislett was practically a financial write-off, even though Asics, her shoe sponsor, also came into the equation with a sizeable bonus for a victory.

But if worst came to worst on Saturday night, Liz, even if she were to lose the race, could count on the minimum wage of £6000 for her quarter of an hour on the track.

On the day of this race, Liz seemed to be in a really black mood. It was evident as soon as she appeared at lunch.

Bislett had laid on a superb buffet. There was everything there. A wonderful range of seafood, lots of meat, vegetables, salad, masses of pasta – because these days every athlete lives on pasta and because there were plenty of Italians competing that night. Like everyone else, the Italians were gobbling it up.

Liz came in with Peter, and they sat on the far side. She looked strained, but they were not late, which meant nothing had run out yet. She had a choice of everything, and there was a lot there.

She called the waiter over. She didn't want what was there, she was asking for something else. The waiter went away and four or five minutes later, when he hadn't returned, she stood up, looked around and left. Then she came back in, picked up two bread rolls, walked out, came back in, picked up a plate to put them on and that was it. It seemed to be a case of pre-race nerves, which Liz acknowledges she suffers from.

By evening there were quite a few people in a tizzy. Steve Cram still held the world record for the mile which he had set at Bislett in 1985, and even though he wasn't running that night because he was injured, and had lost all hope of competing at the Olympics, he was there as a guest of honour.

But an official who didn't recognize him wouldn't let Cram on to the inner circle of track where he was scheduled to address the crowd. Angry, Cram said disdainfully. 'You're what we call in England a "jobsworth".'

Eventually, someone vouched for him, and Steve Cram was able to get to the microphone and wish the crowd every athletic pleasure except that of seeing Steve Cram's world record smashed.

The eyes of the world peer into a runner's soul at Bislett. At this fabled track, the home of the Dream Mile, an arena where an unparalleled fifty-seven world records have been set, the extra-ordinary becomes ordinary. Here the world's first famous female distance runner Grete Waitz had her great days. Here the renowned Ingrid Kristiansen had hers. Liz knows that Kristian-sen's photo is hanging in the gallery of the greats which lines the stairs of Bislett Stadium's main stand. Ingrid has broken records at this track, Liz has only broken Ingrid. Ingrid's six-year-old world 5000-metre record stands. Tonight Liz is going for that record.

Forty-eight hours after Elana Meyer's victory in Stockholm, Liz steps on to the Bislett track. This is the only important race before the Olympics. As she awaits the starter's gun, the eyes in the photograph of Ingrid gaze down at her. Fearfully? Con-temptuously?

To throw down the gauntlet to Elana and the others, to win a battle in the psychological war, Liz needs a fast time today. Fast means finishing in under fifteen minutes. Fast means under Elana's 14 minutes 51.42 seconds in Stockholm. Better still, fast means obliterating Ingrid's 14 minutes 37.33 seconds with a new world record.

The starter's pistol fires. The Italian pace-maker Valentina Tauceri breaks to the front. Liz follows, her face muscles pulled as taut as her bushy blonde hair, already pushing the pace. The first thousand metres is run precisely on target, in 2 minutes 54.73 seconds. Ingrid's world record is within her grasp.

Then Valentina the rabbit turns into a sort of snail, misjudging the pace. A few seconds are lost by two thousand metres, but it is not disaster yet. When Valentina drops out and Liz reaches the end of three thousand metres in 8 minutes 55 seconds flat, the rest of the field is way behind but the race against Ingrid has already been lost.

Putting her head down, Liz hurls herself forward, alone in this stadium of thousands. The crowd claps her on as she completes the fourth kilometre in slightly less than twelve minutes. The race has become a time trial which she can still finish in under fifteen minutes. Her legs look leaden as she crosses the line. Her time of 15 minutes 1.86 seconds is ten seconds slower than Meyer's.

The disappointment shows on Liz's face.

She has won the race, but it is a hollow victory. Meyer ran faster and Kristiansen's world record still stands. Liz has not even run a personal best. To her this victory amounts to defeat. 'I thought I would run better than that.'

What's the matter? What's wrong with her?

'It's getting through to me slowly that I have to ease down a bit more if I am going to run the times I am capable of in Barcelona.' Despite Peter's urging, she hadn't tapered before the race.

The only good news of the evening is that Steve Cram's record still stands.

The Sunday papers bring McColgan no joy. Elana Meyer looked 'sharp' in her race, pronounced the *Independent on Sunday*. 'McColgan looked heavy in comparison.' A dangerous remark. Did the man from the *Indy* mean sluggish or did he mean fat?

A comment like that could have a woman, particularly a runner, looking in the mirror all week.

*

'No one has a divine right to go to the Olympics, and I didn't make the grade,' Daley Thompson says mournfully, announcing his retirement after pulling a hamstring in the first event of the last-ditch decathlon put on specially for him at Crystal Palace. His old mates and his old enemies, including officials he had enjoyed being rude to in his heyday, had hurriedly assembled to give Daley one last try at achieving the Olympic standard. It wasn't to be.

The physical demands made on an athlete's body every day mean there are always pre-Games casualties. Steve Cram was out, so now was Peter Elliott, and Roger Black was on a downhill roll. The British women – Liz and Yvonne and Sally Gunnell – were now among Britain's best gold medal hopes.

Fatima Whitbread, whose arm still hurt whenever she was washing the windows and often when she wasn't, had retired long ago. But as the British team set off for the Olympics, she couldn't help thinking fleetingly of what might have been.

Liz's old rival Ingrid Kristiansen was having very similar thoughts. Her generation's greatest athlete of either sex was slowing down. At the age of thirty-six Ingrid's body was going the way of all athletic flesh. Liz had only just turned twenty-eight.

'Ingrid's recent results,' the other Norwegian Grete Waitz said, deadpan, 'haven't been encouraging.' Waitz had been the world's top female distance runner until Kristiansen came along.

And then along came Liz.

Not surprisingly, Ingrid couldn't find it in her heart to tip Liz as the favourite at the Games. 'Liz McColgan will try to win, but Elana Meyer is the best bet.' On the other hand, Kristiansen covered herself: 'It all depends how Elana makes it through the press and the pressure.' Quite.

Elana Meyer's inexperience *was* the unknown factor. Because South Africa had been ostracized from world sport, she had never run at a major games, never run in the same race as the world's best who were faster and spikier than the local runners Meyer had faced. During the single 5000 metres this summer in Europe, the big guns had stayed away. Would just being at the Olympics overwhelm her?

'She's used to running in the heat, of course,' Waitz interjected.

It would be very hot in Barcelona. 'The only way to beat Liz,' Grete Waitz reasoned aloud, 'is to try to hang on, then outkick her – if you can.'

Kristiansen, however, hoped it would be Liz hanging on. 'Meyer will try to tire everyone before the finish. It will be run the same way as Liz did in Tokyo, but hopefully it will be faster.'

Liz, who never enjoys contemplating the form sheets of her rivals in public, finally did so. There were 'girls' training all over the world who were good and who were out to win it, she said. The girls she would be watching out for most were Lynn Jennings, the American who was her nemesis at cross-country, Germany's Kathrin Ullrich, and, oh yes, Meyer.

'Liz isn't worried,' her mother Betty said astutely the night before Liz left for Barcelona. 'Liz knows she can keep going for ten thousand metres. Can the other girl?' That was precisely the question. It could only be answered at the Games.

Like Liz, Martin Lynch wasn't convinced it was a two-horse race. 'There's at least one Kenyan that's good,' Liz's father told me in May, 'and there is that Ethiopian girl. The one that hung on so long in Tokyo.'

At Gateshead Liz ran a 1500, her last race before the Games. Again she was pipped at the finish by an expert in the distance. Again it was the last lap that had let Liz down.

It had taken guts to run so many races she was likely to lose, to face public defeat solely because those were the races she needed for her Olympic preparation. Some of the media were writing her off. Didn't they know enough about racecraft to understand what she had been doing and give her the credit? Until she had embarked on this course, they had called her Britain's best hope for an Olympic gold medal. Now some of them, like rats, were deserting her Olympic ship.

Elana Meyer, at Gateshead too, racing in the 3000 metres, won in 8 minutes 39.11 seconds, fast, showing off her kick finish. Though in a different race, the extrovert ex-marketing student from Stellenbosch University had sought out Liz McColgan. 'I went up to her to say hello. She just nodded and moved on. Maybe she didn't recognize me.'

Later, at her farewell audience with the media before her departure for the Games, Elizabeth McColgan, the queen of the marathon and the queen of the track, was asked, 'Did you watch Elana Meyer's race?'

'No, why should I?'

'She's going to be one of your main rivals in Barcelona.'

'Everything I need to know about what my chances are,' Liz said, 'I can tell from my own running.'

The follow-up question was: 'Have you spoken to Meyer while you were here?'

'No,' she said. 'Why should I?'

16

This Is Your Life So Far

Barcelona is a city of excess. Big gestures, brimming plates of food and gargantuan scams. The Barcelonans saw the Olympics as a get-rich-quick scheme, and the air-conditioned hotel Kim McDonald had found for Liz and Peter in late April or early May would cost, on prime days, $700 a night. Only the peons among the British track and field athletes who were competing at the Games would be staying at the sweltering Olympic Village.

'The conditions in the village *are* sweaty,' Britain's director of coaching Frank Dick acknowledged. It came as no surprise to him. In the seventy-page *Preparation Report* Frank Dick had sent his athletes months in advance, he had particularly warned endurance athletes like Liz against too many days of pre-competition training in Barcelona because 'air pollution is high'.

The conditions in the village were also cramped, so Dick decided that the athletes, who were being crammed two to a room, each room with one British-team-provided fan, would, on the night before competition, be allowed to sleep in solitary splendour. Of course this meant that for some of those not competing on the morrow their double rooms suddenly became triples.

Arriving in Barcelona ahead of the team, Liz had been met at the airport and shepherded to a hideaway twenty miles away in the seaside resort of Sitges, where she planned to stay until two days before her 1 August heat. She was soon seen skirting tourists and children as she pounded the pinkish pavements of the over-crowded town's streets, forcing her body to adjust to the humidity and the heat.

The two months in cloudy Britain had not been the best physical preparation for acclimatizing to this weather. It had been wintry in June in Sheffield, at Gateshead chillingly windy. This was one overcast British summer in which there had been no jokes about the Costa Blackpool.

Now, with visions of those friendlier hothouses – Tokyo and Tuscaloosa – dancing in her head, Liz began to prepare herself, far away from the loud late-night laughter, the queues and the snoring electric fans that beset the lesser Olympians.

Of the world's superstars, one of the very few staying in the village was Steffi Graf. The multimillionaire tennis player, to whom the world's most luxurious hotel suites were a fact of daily life, had decided to rough it in order to experience the camaraderie of the Games, only to find herself swamped by requests from other Olympians for photos and autographs. Steffi was thinking of moving out at about the same time as Liz, finding the crowded Sitges streets frustratingly unrunnable, was considering moving in ahead of schedule.

Joan Allison, the team manager, told that Liz McColgan wanted a word with her in reception, was surprised to find Liz bags in hand. 'She turned up with all her porridge in her luggage,' said Allison. Liz had decided she needed easy access to the training areas, but she refused the offer of a fan in her room. Sleeping without one, she felt, would help her adapt to the conditions she would face during her showdown with Bondarenko and Elana Meyer.

The main problem of staying in the village was that it would limit her access to Peter. There were very few passes for individual athlete's coaches. But these things have a way of working out. Peter would be there when she needed him.

On Saturday night when Linford Christie, who fortunately had not retired after Tokyo, won his hundred metres gold medal, Liz was in the stadium, too, warming up for her 10,000-metre heat, the preliminary round that would qualify her for the final. To save wear and tear on her calves she had decided to run the heat in trainers instead of racing spikes, a risk but a calculated one. It had worked in Tokyo.

Here she only needed to be one of the first eight runners over the line to make it to the final. As the crowd hugged Linford with its hurrahs, and the screen above the stadium showed him lapping the track in honour, Liz, thinking of her coming race, felt confident she could qualify even without the advantage of spikes.

The object of a heat is to run as slowly as possible, just fast enough to qualify in order to save your energy for the final. Liz was in the first heat, Elana Meyer in the second. Olga Bondarenko, however, was in Liz's heat. Bondarenko had come only third in the Unified Team's Olympic trials, but she might just have been having a bad day as Carl Lewis did at the American trials. Her true current form unknown, Bondarenko was one of the dangers of these Barcelona Olympics.

As the race began, Liz tucked in behind Bondarenko, determined not to lead her anywhere. When the leaders broke away from the pack, Liz went with them and Bondarenko was soon left trailing.

Eyes ahead of her, Liz forgot about the Russian and concentrated on staying up with the winning pack but away from the front. Why waste energy front-running? She finished a comfortable third. The only surprise of the race was that Olga Bondarenko had been running so badly that she realized she couldn't hope to make the final and dropped out. Liz McColgan wouldn't miss her.

Meyer was in the second heat. The diminutive Ethiopian Derartu Tulu, who had hung on for so long in Tokyo, out-sprinted Meyer to the line to win their race. But Tulu had outsprinted Kristiansen in Tokyo in a World Championship heat only to finish the final behind Kristiansen in eighth.

The erstwhile prison administrator from Addis Ababa was the African Games champion, but on a world scale twenty-one-year-old Tulu looked to be a mere 'rabbit', a runner for whom winning the qualifying round was like winning the gold. The BBC pointed out how unnecessary it was for Tulu, who was all of four feet eleven inches tall, to have expended so much energy winning a heat.

Strangely, when a young Briton like Curtis Robb won a heat or a semi-final he was applauded for his mature running. For running his own race. When an African did it, it was called an impulsive blunder. It can be argued that it is good to get into the habit of winning every race. Bad to get out of it. Perhaps that had been the most dangerous thing about Liz's build-up to Barcelona. She was now in the habit of losing.

Liz's pre-race nerves were, on her own admission, often a problem. Peter, as ever, was the best man to calm them. Those deep blue eyes with their understanding twinkle, the softly musical Irish lilt, did not so much ease the tension as tell her that he would always be there, a calm in the face of the storm that was her nature. She knew she gave Peter a lot to contend with, especially before a race. The best thing about him was that he always put her first.

Tonight, at eight-twenty in the evening, British time, she would face the great test of the Olympics.

As they departed for the Montjuic Stadium, as she prepared herself for the twenty-five-lap test, whatever Liz's hopes, whatever her fears, one thing was certain: the tough little girl from the Dundee inner city estate had matured into a strong woman and a great champion. She was queen of the track, and even if someone else were victorious in this race she wouldn't have jewels enough in her crown to dethrone Liz, who was also the heiress apparent to the marathon.

Win or lose Liz would be around for a long, long while. Now, she set her thoughts to the race. If she could climb the Olympic mountain, she would win heaps of glory and a million or more pounds of gold. She would become one of the few British goddesses of sport.

'For me to win tonight is gonna take every ounce of energy that I've got. I'm just gonna run as hard as I possibly can till I drop. I'm gonna give it my all' – she was squinting into the sun – 'and if that's not enough to win, then that's a fact I need to accept.'

Is there any point going through the agony of the race? In hindsight it would appear that even before it Liz sensed defeat. In Tokyo, she had been cocksure. In New York they said Liz lacked respect for the marathon distance when she announced she was going to win. She won both times – and well.

In Barcelona, at the gun Liz went to the front, exactly like

Tokyo – only it was a year later. A general who fights the last war usually finds himself routed. Liz needed to surprise the opposition. Instead she was trying to do it again the same way. She led them round on the first lap in 71.89 seconds. The next laps were 74 and 75 seconds. The pack, a long, lean line with Meyer at the front of it, were close behind her.

The BBC commentators were soon at war. 'I'm surprised they're giving Liz such a smooth ride. I'm surprised Meyer isn't just slipping in front of Liz to let her know she's there.'

'I'd be surprised,' disagreed his other half, 'if she did take it on. She's quite prepared to sit and take a free ride, and so are the rest.'

Liz looked to be in agony, but she often did during a race, so that told us nothing. Meyer made a run for it with nine and a half laps to go, the South Africans in the crowd chanting 'Elana!' Tulu, surprised by the early break, quickly closed the ground between them, but hung back on Meyer's shoulder. Twice Meyer grabbed a sponge from the water station to stave off tiredness and dehydration.

Just before the bell heralding the last lap, Tulu pounced, passing Meyer and sprinting with the gorgeousness of a ballerina to the line. The woman from Addis Ababa became Africa's first Olympic champion. The white African was second.

Liz struggled home in fifth. She felt so tired. Why?

As Tulu prepared to run her lap of honour draped in the flag of Ethiopia, the South African marketing student from Stellenbosch University seized the moment. Covering herself in the Olympic flag, she rushed to join Derartu Tulu. Meyer kissed Tulu on both cheeks, embraced her and grasped her hand. They ran, black and white Africans, hands linked, on the lap of honour. 'Africa could use a couple of stars,' Meyer said. Now Africa had them.

That symbol of African unity which Meyer had engineered made the front page of *The Times*. Liz's defeat had become a victory for African unity. It was unlikely Liz would take much comfort.

Even in defeat, Liz graced the front pages of the *Telegraph* and the *Express* and the back page of most of the rest. Her defeat was big news, perhaps bigger than Sally Gunnell's gold medal. It touched more hearts. There had been more people watching Liz's race on television than had tuned in for Linford's. John Major had been in the stadium.

One bad race, even a very important one, does not a reputation unmake. Famous victories, though, do wonders. Gwen Torrence won two golds in Barcelona. Liz none. But then she surprised us with a late-season world triumph.

Liz wants to be the greatest female distance runner ever. She has designed her life around that dream, and at the age of twenty-eight she is well on the way to achieving it. Olympic silver medallist in Seoul, world champion in Tokyo, multi-world-record holder with a fistful of British and Commonwealth titles, she surprised everyone but herself by winning the lauded and lucrative New York Marathon in her marathon debut. That was a good race.

As for the Barcelona final, 'It was just a bad race. I couldn't breathe very well, she said afterwards. I'm disappointed. My legs were tingly. My legs are cramping up even now. It must be dehydration.' To some of us she had been looking anaemic all season, a problem for many distance runners. At last, she was going to go for tests to see if there was anything wrong.

Three weeks after the Olympics Liz had the answer. Her problem was anaemia. Iron deficiency anaemia makes ordinary mortals feel lethargic. Liz found herself unable to run in high gear anywhere near her best. Anaemia could explain her feelings of breathlessness in Barcelona because iron helps transport the oxygen in blood. All season long, single-minded Liz had been training despite feeling fatigued.

'I knew in myself there was something wrong. I was very tired. I trained too hard too soon,' she realizes now.

Instead of resting after Tokyo, Liz had trained for a marathon. Then in the first two months of 1992 she had pushed herself to set world bests at 5000 metres and in the half marathon. No wonder that by March, run down, anaemic and therefore virus-prone, she had that world cross-country disaster presaging a disappointing season. But think of it, fifth in the Olympics while anaemic. The woman is a wonder.

It took another three weeks of treatment – iron in combination with vitamin C – to return Liz to form. She won a few minor races, and then a big one. On 20 September 1992, Liz McColgan became the first ever women's world half-marathon champion. She is the only British athlete, male or female, ever to win two world championship titles.

No more anaemias, Liz promises. 'I'm going to give myself more self-respect and listen to my body.'

But don't expect her to train any less single-mindedly. It just wouldn,t be Liz. Her famous single-mindedness is akin to her penchant for speaking her mind. Both excellent traits if you are Nigel Mansell or Botham or Gatting. But if you're a woman you had better watch out. There are many out there who prefer you to be mealy-mouthed.

Peter, whose manners and manner are charming in the best sense of that word, often intercedes on her behalf. Liz herself does not suffer fools, and there are some who do not count themselves fools who have felt scorned.

A very private person, Liz can be abrupt with strangers. It can even be argued – in fact I do argue – that she needs to be. Otherwise she would be swamped by requests and distractions. Dealing with the pressures of being a renowned champion is difficult.

Getting the balance right is hard. Sometimes impossible. So, like Britain's other famous Elizabeth, Elizabeth Lynch McColgan has her detractors as well as her many admirers. To old friends and to family there is evidence that she is generous and good. But epithets like aloof and abrasive have been used about her. In print she has been called a loner, even 'a Jekyll and Hyde'. To her detractors the queen of the track seems neither regal nor imperial; merely imperious.

Is she arrogant? Or just plain shy? Can it be that Liz Lynch McColgan is simply unswervingly single-minded? Is this a fault, or a concomitant of her achievement? Of her greatness?

There is no one-sentence answer to what makes Liz run. But when all is said and done, Liz McColgan is a great British heroine. And they are a rare and precious breed.

*

The sandy-haired young Dundee cab driver kept the secret when he overheard the *This Is Your Life* producer and the Grampian executive talking in his cab. If Liz found out, they told him, the *This Is Your Life* programme about her would be axed.

It is not till a month later that the phone rings in Vi Bennett's house. It is Sarah Ann Cockcroft of *This Is Your Life*. 'We are thinking of doing a programme about Liz McColgan,' Cockcroft says.

'That's wonderful, love,' Vi says, her voice rising in excitement.

'I am calling in confidence,' Cockcroft tells Vi. 'If Liz McColgan finds out about the programme, we will cancel it.'

'I promise I won't say a word to anyone.'

'That's what we usually advise,' Cockcroft says.

Vi's telephone is in the foyer. There is a knock on the door. It is a couple of friends popping in. A look of alarm invades Vi's face. 'I'll be with you in a wee moment,' she says abruptly, returning to her phone call. She seems unhappy to see them. That's not a bit like Vi.

As the worried visitors sit on the plump sofa waiting for her to finish her call, they overhear the odd, mysterious word, and when Vi comes in to the room they ask her, 'What is it, love? What is wrong, Vi?'

'It's nothing wrong. It's just a wee shock,' she finally confesses. 'That was a girl from *This Is Your Life*. They are doing a programme about Liz.' Vi swears them to secrecy. They too keep the secret.

Betty Lynch had far more of a problem. She was seeing Liz every day. On the night, a Grampian anniversary party was used to lure Liz to Caird Hall. As she was getting ready to go, her mother was in rather a state. Betty was on a tight timetable.

The limousine waited while Liz kissed Eilish goodnight. It was Eilish's grandmother who had undressed her and got her ready for bed. Liz went to say goodbye to her mother and to show herself off. With her glamorous new hairstyle and the long lean trousers, she looked like a million bucks.

Betty Lynch, hiding in the bathroom, all dressed and fully made-up, called out, 'I'm in the bath. Have a good time.'

When the limousine pulled out of the driveway Betty was already buttoning Eilish into her frilly white dress.

Minutes after their daughter's departure, the Lynches and their granddaughter were on their way. When she arrived at Caird Hall, Betty handed over the baby and rushed on to the stage. She didn't have time to say hello to anyone, let alone have a steadying cup of tea. If you knew her you could just see she was shattered. But as the television audience didn't, she seemed fine.

Liz couldn't believe it when Michael Aspel appeared.

'I'm not old enough. I'm not good enough,' she said.

'But you've done quite a lot,' said Aspel. 'World Champion Liz McColgan, tonight this is your life.'

And the show went on. With all the great sporting moments – Edinburgh, Seoul, Tokyo and the marathon through the sky-scraper canyons of New York. With all of the touching personal sidelights – Liz running into her dad's arms and being lifted into the air immediately after her Edinburgh Commonwealth Games triumph; Liz, the new world champion weeping with emotion on the victory podium in Tokyo.

The people important to Liz were there. Her teacher Phil Kearns remembered her first race and her continuing visits to St Saviour's to encourage the pupils. Vi Bennett was there and Kirsty Wade, and her whole family, of course, and Peter's. There was even a video from America of Coach John Mitchell with some of the British athletes Liz had recommended to him. They were doing well.

At the end of the programme Michael Aspel held the famous red book out to her. Amending the programme's famous closing line, the line in the written script, he now said, 'This, so far, is your life, Elizabeth McColgan.'

He is right. We will see a lot more of her yet.